D0343107

Wanted!

DUMB or ALIVE

Wanted! DUMB or ALIVE

100 NEW STORIES FROM THE FILES OF AMERICA'S DUMBEST CRIMINALS®

DANIEL BUTLER and ALAN RAY

Illustrations by Mike Harris

RUTLEDGE HILL PRESS

Nashville, Tennessee

Published in Nashville, Tennessee, by Rutledge Hill Press, 211 Seventh Avenue North, Nashville, Tennessee 37219.

Distributed in Canada by H. B. Fenn & Company, Ltd., 34 Nixon Road, Bolton, Ontario L7E 1W2.

Distributed in New Zealand by Tandem Press, 2 Rugby Road, Birkenhead, Auckland 10.

Distributed in the United Kingdom by Verulam Publishing, Ltd., 152a Park Street Lane, Park Street, St. Albans, Hertfordshire AL2 2AU.

Typography by E. T. Lowe, Nashville, Tennessee

Special contributions by Don Parker and Mac Bennett

Library of Congress Cataloging-in-Publication Data

Butler, Daniel R., 1951–
    Wanted! dumb or alive : 100 new stories from the files of
  America's dumbest criminals / Daniel Butler and Alan Ray ;
  Illustrations by Mike Harris.
      p. cm.
   ISBN 1-55853-421-0 (pbk.)
    1. Crime—United States—Case studies.   2. Criminals—United
States—Case studies.   3. Crime—United States—Humor.   I. Ray,
Alan. II. Title.
HV6783.B875   1996
364.1'092'273—dc20
{B}   96-32030
                                          CIP

Printed in the United States of America

3   4   5   6   7   8   9—99   98   97

To God, our loving families, and
our friends—in that order

Introduction

Hello. I'm Alan Ray, and he's Daniel Butler. One day we got this crazy idea to write a book about true stories of dumb criminals. Not in our wildest collective dreams did we envision the amount of time, money, laughter, sacrifice, and hard work it would take to bring this quest to fruition.

We were prepared to accept the fact there might not be that many stories out there. What we weren't prepared for was the salvo of funny, absurd, and oftentimes unbelievable stories we would ultimately uncover and put into our first book, which we titled *America's Dumbest Criminals*. We were in awe, and we are still. That book went on to be a surprise bestseller. And it brought to us even more amazing true stories from policemen and policewomen all over the country—one hundred of which appear in the pages of this second book.

The last year has been an incredible time for us. The months and months on the road, the thousands of miles we traveled, our patient families at home, and the hundreds of good people we've been blessed to have met all serve to remind us that the truest reward isn't found in the destination, but in the journey. This journey has given back more in experience, memories, and stories we could tell than it ever took out in the many lean days and sleepless nights we spent trying to make it happen.

Like interviewing seventy-five-year-old retired cop Hi Powell, who once smacked Bugsy Siegel upside the head when Bugsy offered him a bribe. Once, when we were on the road doing a book signing in conjunction with a phone-in radio interview in Birmingham, Alabama, we got a call from a guy in prison listening to the show. He was doing fifteen years for something. He told us a couple of stories, we told him a few, and we all laughed together. Before he hung up, he requested an autographed copy of the book. We figured he probably wouldn't make the book signing the next night (at least, we hoped he wouldn't), so we sent him a signed copy. We were very happy that he had called in because it told us that he understood the humor of it all.

We certainly learned a lot about *dumb criminals*. For one thing, it's a club anyone can join. In fact, if memory serves, one time we were on our way to Pensacola, Florida, to do some interviews. It was probably four in the morning, and we were absolutely fried. We were on a two-lane highway, running sixty miles per hour in heavy fog, when suddenly—I guess we'd reached some little town—the road forked sharply. You could go right, or you could go left. I went straight. I mashed on the brake pedal while giving the seat a hickey at the same time. Daniel awoke from his coma long enough to mutter a catatonic "uh-oh" as we skidded fifty feet to a sideways stop in a parking lot. We were sitting in the parking lot of the Alabama state police headquarters!

Our heads slowly turned toward each other at the same time, like a ventriloquist and his dummy. "Wanna get some stories while we're here?" we asked in unison. We were awake after that and we laughed all the way to Florida. Live and learn.

We've spoken with so many wonderful people we could write a book on just the insightful thoughts and philosophies that policemen and policewomen around the country have shared with us. (Let me make a note of that.) We hope that this second collection of stories about America's dumbest criminals will give you just a taste of what we've experienced.

As in the first book, none of the dumb crimes depicted is still under adjudication. None of the criminals is identified by his or her real name, and some details have been changed to protect the privacy of the people involved. But all the stories are real and so are the cops who appear in this book. We use their real names with their permission. We are especially grateful to Don Parker and Mac Bennett for going above and beyond the call of duty in providing us with so many great stories. Thanks, guys!

It really has been a wild ride—and as far as we can see, it's not over yet. So to God, our families, our friends, the police, our publisher, and to you, we say: Thanks for the journey. We'll see you along the way.

Wanted!
DUMB or ALIVE

WARNING:
THE CRIMES YOU ARE ABOUT TO READ ARE TRUE.
THE NAMES HAVE BEEN CHANGED ...
TO PROTECT THE IGNORANT.

The Bagman Cometh

Disguises often cause dumb criminals a lot of problems. Such was the case with the would-be robber who, according to Lt. John Hutchinson of Little Rock, Arkansas, was captured on surveillance camera video.

It seems our burglar had a carefully thought-out plan to rob an electronics store, but he forgot about his all-important disguise. So just before he entered the store, he grabbed a plastic bag and yanked it down over his head. Mind you, this was not a clear plastic bag, but the opaque garbage variety, and our suspect didn't take the time to cut out eyeholes.

Roll tape, and we see our antihero on surveillance video stumbling through the electronics store, falling over television sets and even tripping an alarm system on display. Finally, he falls to the floor, nearly suffocating on his plastic bag, and crawls to an exit.

But he's back minutes later, this time with two eyeholes cut out. This time he succeeds in grabbing more than sixteen hundred dollars' worth of electronic gear and getting away with all of it, scot-free.

Or so it seems.

After the police stopped laughing at the surveillance footage, they noticed that below the Bagman's clever disguise was a security guard's uniform complete with nametag. He was, they cleverly deduced, the mall security guard who was on duty at the time.

Sure enough, the security guard was setting up his new entertainment center at his apartment when the police arrived. Judging from this brilliant man's past history, we would not be surprised if he came back to rob the store again with a full-length, clear-plastic dry-cleaning bag to cover his uniform.

They're Gonna Get Ya

Detective Jerry Wiley of Birmingham, Alabama, has been involved in a lot of sting operations in his time, but none as outrageously successful as this one. It came about because his department was holding almost three thousand outstanding warrants for crimes ranging from parking violations to assault. Sending out warrant officers to track down each offender and serve each warrant would have taken thousands of man-hours and probably years. So the department decided that instead of going to the criminals, they would get the criminals to come to them.

Here's the sting setup: The police department put together a sports channel for the local cable system—on paper only. The letterhead and promotional brochure bore the phony sports channel's logo, WGGY, which, by the way, stood for "We're Gonna Get Ya." The president of WGGY was "J. L. Byrd," who sent out a letter to each offender explaining that he or she was "already a winner!" All the "winners" had to do was show up at a selected site at a certain time on the day of the drawing for an all-expenses-paid vacation to New Orleans.

The cops had no idea how many people would respond. Commercial direct-mail marketers consider a 10 percent response a huge success for promotions of this type. But on the day of the drawing, the police were stunned to see more than four hundred people already lined up waiting to claim their tickets and win the trip to New Orleans.

All the "winners" were asked to present a photo I.D. and informed that family members could not accompany them into the room where the drawing would be held. They would be processed in groups of twenty-five at a time. (The small groups were necessary to keep the crowd manageable and insure that no one would be injured.)

To keep the crowd entertained and involved as people were slowly being processed, Wiley took a video camera down the waiting line and interviewed the lucky "winners." He even asked some of them to do promos for the new sports channel. Looking right into the camera, dumb criminal after dumb criminal said, "WGGY got me. Did they get you yet?" Meanwhile, the people ahead of them were inside getting the surprise of their lives.

As each group sat down in the winners' room with

Looking right into the camera, dumb criminal after dumb criminal said, "WGGY got me. Did they get you yet?"

their fingers crossed and their hopes high, President J. L. Byrd (actually, a detective from vice) stood behind the podium and explained the drawing. "We're about to give you your tickets and have the drawing for the trip to New Orleans. But first, we have one more surprise for you."

At that instant, the doors burst open with armed S.W.A.T. team officers surrounding the "winners," who immediately put up their hands in utter shock and disbelief. Since it was impossible to pat down the offenders for weapons, the appearance of the S.W.A.T. officers was so sudden that nobody even thought of responding.

The sting succeeded in taking more than four hundred criminals off the streets, collecting more than ten thousand dollars in fines, and saving the city thousands of dollars in door-to-door searches and warrant serving. Not a bad day's work.

Photo Finish

Officer Aaron Graham of Louisville, Kentucky, likes to tell this story of a crime with a photo finish. It began with a woman strolling through a park en route to a company picnic. Swinging from her shoulder was her trusty Polaroid camera, all loaded and ready to catch some candid shots of this wacky annual summer get-together. The sun was setting, and the sky was ablaze with color as a breeze cooled the evening air. It was one of those relaxing evenings when you can't help but let your guard down just a little.

Suddenly, she heard running footsteps. Someone jerked the woman's arm and grabbed the camera. A patrol officer responded to the woman's screams and set out on foot in pursuit of the young thieves. While he ran, he radioed in a physical description of the perpetrators and their general direction of flight.

Meanwhile, in a small wooded grove not a quarter of a mile away, the thieves were checking out the camera. But something was wrong. They took each other's pictures easily enough, but the film that emerged from the camera was black. Disgusted, they tossed the photos and headed for the pawnshop to see what they could get for the malfunctioning camera.

Several police units and several bicycle and horse-mounted officers were close behind, forming a perimeter as our foot patrol officer stumbled into the grove of trees. There, lying at his feet, were the quickly developing Polaroid photos of the culprits. The officer knew he must be less than a minute behind them because the developing process was just finishing.

The two boys were nabbed about a half-mile away as they photographed squirrels. But they were still having problems. They would shoot a photo, look at it, and toss it down, grumbling, "Darn camera doesn't work!"

The trail of photos they left behind worked better than a trail of bread crumbs.

The Name Game

4

Officer Ed Leach of Birmingham, Alabama, likes to tell the tale of two brothers, Jack and Joe, who greatly resembled each other in both physical appearance and their less-than-brilliant behavior.

Jack and Joe were often getting into trouble of one sort or another, only to weasel their way out of sticky situations by switching identities. If one got nabbed for doing something wrong, the innocent one would use the other's name to get out of trouble. The ploy usually worked, until Officer Leach decided to turn the tables while trying to issue an outstanding warrant on Jack.

On patrol one afternoon, Leach spotted Joe at a stoplight and pulled him over, hoping to get some information on Jack's whereabouts. It so happened that Leach knew Jack and Joe well enough to tell the two apart, even from a distance.

After Leach had stepped out of his car to speak to Joe, he happened to spot Jack nearby, walking across the street. Although Leach and Jack made eye contact, Jack just kept on walking as though nothing was wrong. Time for a little reverse psychology.

"I was on to their little game of mistaken identities, so I thought I'd give them a taste of their own medicine," Leach remembers. "I knew if I called out his real name, Jack would start running. So I didn't. Instead, I called out the name of his brother—who was standing beside me.

" 'Hey, Joe!' I yelled. 'Come over here and talk to me, would ya?' "

Now Jack, fooled into thinking that Officer Leach thought *he* was Joe, walked right up to Leach, who then grabbed the real jerk, er, Jack, by the shirt.

"You're under arrest, *Jack,*" Leach said.

"Hey . . . but I thought that you thought . . . that I was. . . . Damn! Man, that's not right."

Jack knew he'd been had, and he didn't like it one bit. He had fallen for his own game.

It Never Dawned on Him

5

The Las Vegas dawn sky was gray and the first rays of sunlight were peeking over the desert mountains. Officer Gordon Martines was routinely working the red-eye shift when a car roared past him at sixty-five miles per hour in a thirty-five zone. Martines took off in hot pursuit.

After he had pulled his lead-footed prey off to the side of the road, Officer Martines exited his car. The man stepped out of his and walked toward Martines in an obvious state of nervousness, gazing toward the desert and the brightening horizon.

"I know you're not going to believe me," he told Martines, "but I'm a vampire, and I've got to get back to my coffin before the sun comes up!"

"Okay," Martines said, a brow arched. "I'll write this real quick so you can get going."

The guy was back in his car and out of sight before the sun appeared, so Officer Martines never saw if the man really was a vampire . . . or just plain batty.

6 As Innocent as a Baby

Retired police captain Don Parker of Pensacola, Florida, knows as well as anyone that mistakes are sometimes made when it comes to enforcing the law. That appeared to be the case in an apparent shoplifting incident. When the policeman arrived on the scene at the security office of a large department store, he saw a young mother with an infant in a stroller. The woman was crying her eyes out as two store security people looked on.

"But I keep telling you, I didn't do nothing," she wailed as tears streamed down her cheeks.

The police officer asked the head of store security to step outside to discuss the case in private. The woman was suspected of stealing several gold chains, but no evidence had been uncovered during a search of the woman and the diaper bag. "I know she's got them someplace," the security guard muttered. "I just have to find them."

Back inside, the woman was still weeping. "I ain't got

Suddenly, his hand went down into his diaper and came out clutching three gold chains.

nothing to hide," she said tearfully. "I just want to take my baby and go home." The baby was starting to whimper, and the woman bent down to kiss him. "Now don't you fuss, darlin'. We'll be going home soon."

She began repacking the diaper bag as the baby continued to whine, plucking at his diaper and squirming in the stroller. Suddenly, his hand went down into his diaper and came out clutching three gold chains. He flung them onto the floor and went back for more.

By the time it was over, nine expensive gold chains had been recovered. The mother watched in grim-faced silence as the chains were gathered up, but as soon as the officer started reading her Miranda rights to her, she exploded.

"I hope you're not thinking about arresting me," she spat out. The officer replied that this was exactly what he had in mind. She shook her head and pointed at the infant. "He's the one who stole the chains," she said huffily. "I didn't do anything!"

Roll Call for Criminals

Getting a sincere confession of guilt that is admissible in court is often difficult, but when it happens, the sense of satisfaction makes up for all the lean times.

One such case in the Southwest involved two men on trial for armed robbery and assault. You could hear a pin drop in the courtroom as the prosecutor questioned the victim, who, along with her husband, had been robbed at gunpoint. Her voice quavered, and she seemed terribly frightened. Noting this, the prosecutor raised his voice and turned his gaze away from the woman, hoping not to intimidate her any further.

"Are the two men who committed this horrible crime in the courtroom today?" he sternly asked.

At that, the two defendants raised their hands. The courtroom gallery and even the judge snickered. Noticing the two arms in the air, the prosecutor said, "Your honor, may the record show that the defendants raised their hands and have just confessed to the crime."

8 The Not-So Good Samaritans

One chilly winter night in Birmingham, Alabama, officer Anthony Parks received a call that an apartment burglary was in progress. When Parks got there, the residents greeted him and explained that they had the burglar in custody. Sure enough, the culprit was sitting at the kitchen table finishing off a hamburger. This deserved an explanation.

It seems that our apartment residents had made a burger run to a nearby drive-through. When they returned, they noticed that their apartment door had been jimmied and was partially open. They immediately called 911 and then surprised the crook going through their closets. He tried to explain:

"Well, it was so cold out there tonight, and I don't have any place to stay. So I broke in just to get warm and maybe take a warmer jacket for the long, cold night ahead."

The burglar's sob story touched the apartment

dwellers' hearts. So they shared their burgers with the burglar and gave him a denim jacket. The victims actually pleaded with Parks to not arrest their unfortunate burglar. But the law is the law, and this chilly willy had broken it, so it was off to the booking room.

"We always pat down and search the prisoners when they're being booked, and that's what I was doing to this poor man when I made an amazing discovery," Parks said. "He was in possession of a quantity of crack cocaine. And this was as much a surprise to him as it was to me, because I found it in the pocket of the denim jacket that his victims had just given him. Possession is still nine-tenths of the law, so I had to book him for possession of cocaine. But at least he spent the night in a warm jail cell."

Every good deed deserves another, so the Birmingham police paid a return visit to the not-so-good Samaritans who were themselves booked after a search of the apartment turned up drugs and drug paraphernalia.

9 Parlez-vous Français?

The small town of Phoenix in upstate New York is only ninety miles from the Canadian border, and occasional language problems crop up with the French-speaking neighbors to the north.

Deputy Bill Cromie was on routine patrol one evening when a big Cadillac with Ontario plates zipped by. He stopped the car and asked the driver for his license. Speaking in French, the man indicated that he didn't understand. Cromie made some hand signals to indicate he wanted the man's driver's license, but the driver just shook his head.

"Right from the start, I had the idea that he understood a lot more than he was admitting," Cromie says. "After all, even in Canada, the first thing a cop is going to ask for during a traffic stop is the driver's license."

Cromie attempted to explain that he was going to write the man a ticket for speeding and that he would have to make an immediate appearance before the judge. The guy shook his head the entire time, and Cromie was beginning to get irritated at what he was convinced was nothing more than a charade.

"Sir, do you know what a *bastille* is?" Cromie finally asked.

"You give me ticket?" the man said, finally breaking his silence in barely understandable English.

"Oh, it will be much better than that," Cromie said. "You're going to get to meet our judge."

"I no understand."

Nevertheless, the man was soon standing in front of the judge, who read the charges to him—in English. The guy shrugged helplessly and in fractured English indicated that he didn't understand. Looking as pitiful as he could make himself look, the driver rattled off a long response in French. The judge waited until he finished, nodded politely, and in perfect French repeated the charges. Then he informed him—again in French—that the fine would be a hundred dollars.

"A hundred dollars!" the driver yelped in clear and understandable English. Realizing his error, he quickly reverted to his garbled speech again, but it was too late.

"Yes, the fine will be a hundred dollars," the bilingual judge repeated with a smile, "U.S. currency only."

Bad Excuse No. 53

Most folks probably have been stopped for speeding at one time or another and are usually ready with a perfectly good excuse for breaking the law. Sgt. Johnny Cooley of Birmingham, Alabama, has worked traffic on the local interstate highway for almost a quarter of a century, but the creative excuses he hears never cease to amaze him—as was the case with the following, which occurred just as rush-hour traffic on a Friday afternoon was starting to hit full stride.

Sergeant Cooley popped on his radar gun and sat back in his cruiser. It was a beautiful afternoon. Maybe this would be one afternoon rush hour that would just roll on smoothly like the swiftly setting sun. No such luck.

Within moments, Cooley's radar gun screamed. When he checked the speed, the gun read "102." That's one hundred two miles per hour in a fifty-five-mile-per-hour speed zone! The car blew by in the left lane, and Cooley peeled out behind with lights and siren on. Three miles down the road, he had the speeder pulled off to the shoulder.

"I always ask the motorists first why they were speeding, because you never know when someone's in the middle of a real emergency and might need help," Cooley says. "The last thing I want to do is impede someone who has a legitimate medical emergency. So I asked him if he had a problem."

The driver was very calm and almost sheepish when he answered Cooley, "Uh, no . . . no, sir."

"So I asked him why he was going one hundred two miles per hour in a fifty-five speed zone."

"Well, I just got my car washed and I . . . uh . . . well, I was trying to blow-dry it," the guy said.

Cooley asked him how much the car wash had cost him. The driver looked confused but told the officer "five bucks."

"So I handed him the ticket and told him the blow-dry was going to cost him one hundred twenty-five dollars."

11 Paging All Dumb Crooks

Officer Aaron Graham is the media information officer for the Louisville (Kentucky) Police Department. His job is to issue press releases regarding his department's arrests, investigations, personnel changes, and events, and he tries to answer any questions the media might have. Sometimes the hardened reporters who cover headquarters and review the police blotter have a hard time believing Graham's press releases. But occasionally the truth about dumb criminals defies even Officer Graham's imagination.

Graham recounted for us in detail the story of an officer in his department who got a call saying there had been a house break-in and that several items were missing from the house. So he responded and, well, it gets pretty unbelievable from there on.

The officer was taking down a laundry list of items stolen along with descriptions, serial numbers, and values when the owner of the house noticed that his son's beeper had been taken. Just on a lark, the officer called the beeper number. Within moments, the thief was calling the house that he had just robbed an hour and a half earlier. The owner of the house also had caller I.D. on his telephone, so now the thief's name and phone number were scrolling across the little LCD screen. The owner kept him in conversation.

"No, I didn't beep you. It must've been my son, and he's in the shower. Are you at home?"

"Yes, sir."

"Well, could you try back in about five minutes? He should be out by then."

"Okay."

Five minutes later, true to his word, he called back. By this time the officers had discovered where he lived— just a few blocks away. The victim was still talking to the robber on the phone when the police burst into the robber's house and apprehended him with the stolen beeper in his hand.

"Paging Mr. Knucklehead. Mr. Knucklehead, you have a call . . ."

12 Collar around the Ring

One jewel thief learned the hard way that diamonds aren't *really* forever. Providence, Rhode Island, police chief William Devine explains:

"The suspect wasn't really a jewel thief. He was really just a shoplifter who bit off a little more than he could chew," Devine said.

It seems our two-bit thief had gone into a jewelry store and asked to see some diamond rings. The clerk obliged him and brought out a tray of the store's largest, most expensive pieces. Our would-be jewel thief tried on just about every ring in the place but just couldn't find the right one. He was about to give up and leave when the clerk noticed that one of the rings, the most expensive one, was missing. Naturally, the clerk mentioned this.

The thief was outraged at what obviously was an accusation directed at him. He denied any knowledge of the ring and accused the clerk of trying to pull a fast one. The clerk called the police anyway and, just before the

Just before the cops arrived, she noticed her "customer" pop
something into his mouth.

cops arrived, she noticed her "customer" pop something into his mouth.

The police had a good idea that the man was in possession of the stolen ring, but they couldn't find it on him. Maybe it was *in* him. So they decided to search the suspect internally.

Sure enough, an x ray of the suspect's abdomen showed a ring cuddling up against the ham sandwich he had eaten for lunch an hour earlier. But before the jewelry store owner could positively identify the ring, everyone had to wait for nature to take its course.

Like sands through the hourglass, the ring did materialize in due time. And, yes, it was the stolen one. The man was booked and convicted.

We just had to ask about the method of evidence retrieval used by the police in this case. But all Chief Devine would say about it was, "That job went to the officer who was low man on the totem pole."

DUMB CRIMINAL QUIZ NO. 111

How well do you know the dumb criminal mind?

Suppose that you and two dumb criminal friends have just escaped from an American prison near the Mexican border. You swim across the Rio Grande River, and you're safely into Mexico when you realize that your pickup man hasn't shown up yet. Do you and your friends . . .

a) Swim back across the Rio Grande into the States to find a phone and get arrested by the state police?

b) Split up and go your own separate ways?

c) Find a place to hide and wait for him?

HINT: Remember. You're not just criminals, you're dumb criminals.

Of course, the answer could only be (a). Believe it or not, that was the choice that the real three amigos made!

13 Ant That a Shame?

Capt. Arnetta Nunn of Birmingham, Alabama, got a "disturbing the peace" call in her rookie days that turned out to be somewhat odd. She rolled on the call, but when she arrived at the address, she couldn't hear anything unusual. No deafening music. No loud voices. No noise. Nothing. She was about to call back the person who had made the complaint, when two men ran out of the house and hotfooted it through the yard.

"Law-abiding citizens don't run from the police, so my partner and I pursued the two males on foot," Nunn says. "My partner grabbed one of them almost immediately, but my guy was a little faster. He turned a corner and darted behind a neighbor's house just a few feet ahead of me. When I came around the corner, he had disappeared. I looked everywhere, but the guy had just vaporized."

Nunn prided herself on her running speed, and she just couldn't believe she had lost this guy. Then she noticed that the bushes up against the house were shaking, just a little at first, but then more violently. She pointed her gun at the bushes.

"All right, come on out with your hands in the air!" she yelled.

Sure enough, the culprit stepped out, but he couldn't keep his hands in the air. He would scratch his back and chest frantically and then put them into the air again.

"It seems the man had lain down right in a nest of fire ants, and they were eating him alive. It's a good thing. I might never have found him if the ants hadn't helped out."

14 Sorry about That

Officer Dan Newman of the Las Vegas (Nevada) Police Department told America's Dumbest Criminals of an unintentionally funny event that occurred while he was involved in a routine narcotics operation.

"We raided the house of a known drug dealer, and the suspect, upon our entering, went running down a hallway toward the back of the home," Newman said. "Unbeknownst to us, the man was an amputee who usually wore a prosthesis. After a moment or two of hide-and-seek, my partner yelled out from the back of the house, 'Hey, I've got the suspect here in the back bedroom . . . and he's unarmed!' "

It wasn't until Newman and his partner entered the room and saw the prosthetic limb lying on the bed that they realized the true impact of the statement. Even the suspect laughed—but not for long. He was arrested for possession of a controlled substance with the intent of resale.

Robbery Returns

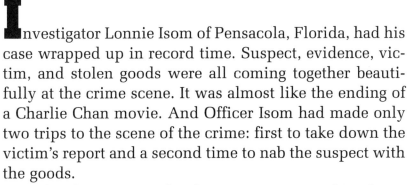

Investigator Lonnie Isom of Pensacola, Florida, had his case wrapped up in record time. Suspect, evidence, victim, and stolen goods were all coming together beautifully at the crime scene. It was almost like the ending of a Charlie Chan movie. And Officer Isom had made only two trips to the scene of the crime: first to take down the victim's report and a second time to nab the suspect with the goods.

On his first visit to the shopping center parking lot, a woman had reported to him that someone had broken into her car and stolen some merchandise that she had just purchased at an electronics store. This is an all-too-common call, and the clues were few to none, but Isom made as detailed a report as possible and began to check on other thefts in the area and links to the usual suspects.

He needn't have bothered. Less than twenty-four hours later, the woman called back and asked Isom to come quickly to the electronics store. He arrived to find her holding a suspect, assisted by an off-duty deputy and a clerk.

It seems that the woman had returned to the store to find out the exact value of the items for her insurance claim. While she was trying to describe what she had bought, a man came in to ask for a refund on several items.

"I had one like that! And that! Wait, those are mine!" she cried.

The thief was trying to return her stolen things right in front of her!

Isom, in his best Perry Mason-Charlie Chan investigative style, laid out the crime when he arrived. "*You* stole *these* items which *she* purchased at *this* store. *You* took them from *her* car in *that* parking lot and were trying to return them for money at the *same* store while *she* was trying to determine their value."

Everything sure seemed to jibe, and there was no way to deny the obvious, so the suspect didn't try. But later that night, when Isom was questioning him at the jail, the thief with the bad timing complained that someone had stolen his soap and towel from his cell.

The Fall to Grace

Sgt. Johnny Cooley was running radar on the interstate outside Birmingham, Alabama, one night when he witnessed a bona fide traffic miracle.

The street was slick from a rain that had just ended, and the pace of traffic was again picking up. An eighteen-wheeler came barreling around a curve, when a car suddenly switched lanes directly into the truck's path. The truck driver hit the brakes and began to hydroplane across the lanes, out of control. The cab of the truck hit the railing at full speed and the trailer followed, disappearing over the edge of an overpass.

Cooley knew there was a basketball court below, and chances were real good that a pickup game was in progress. Cooley quickly radioed in for paramedics and backup. When he got to the twisted, crushed semi, his worst fears surfaced, although it appeared that the basketball players had escaped: they were all busy looting the trailer of its beer and wine haul. When they saw Cooley, they made a fast break toward the shadows.

Sergeant Cooley sighed as he stepped out of his cruiser for the worst part of his job—visually confirming the traffic fatality. He stepped up on what was left of the cab's running board and peered into a small opening that used to be the driver's side window. He gritted his teeth and swallowed hard. But when he looked in, he couldn't believe his eyes. There was a woman lying comfortably stretched out on the seat, reading a book.

"Ma'am? Are you okay?"

The woman calmly closed her book and smiled, "Oh, I'm fine, thank you."

Cooley could not believe that she had survived the crash, much less the sixty-five-foot drop.

"Were you driving the rig, ma'am?"

She smiled again, "Yes, sir, but I had some help."

"Help? You mean another driver? Where is he? The paramedics are here."

"My copilot's right here," she said, holding up the Bible she had been reading. "God."

Granted, the only dummies in this story were the freeloading basketballers, but it's a story that just had to be told.

Not Quite Clever Enough

17

A young man in Pensacola, Florida, was enterprising enough to "acquire" a woman's purse.

He was also clever enough to forge the woman's signature on a note saying: "It's my son's birthday, and I am too sick to get out of bed. Please let my son spend up to five hundred dollars. Thanks very much."

Our young entrepreneur went to a department store and purchased a lot of nice clothes and some really cool shoes. He signed the charge slip, gave the lady his *real* home phone number, and went merrily on his way.

The police were having a nice chat with his *real* mom by the time he got his packages home.

18 Be Careful How You Choose Your Friends

Dumb criminals come in all shapes and sizes as well as personality types. Some are quiet, some are shy, some are talkative, and some are downright friendly. When Bill Page was an Illinois state trooper, he ran into one of the friendly ones. Not necessarily smart, but definitely friendly.

It all happened during a long and boring midnight shift in a small rural Illinois county. Around four in the morning, Page stopped at a local restaurant for breakfast. He sat with a couple of deputy acquaintances, and as they were talking they saw a pickup truck pull into the parking lot. The driver got out, and all three lawmen recognized him immediately. He was a local thief named Jim who had been in and out of trouble most of his life.

The man walked into the restaurant, spotted the three cops, and came over to chat. They talked for a few minutes, and Jim finally walked off. Looking at the truck through the window of the restaurant, the three diners noticed that it had a company logo painted on the door. One of the deputies called the manager of the company who owned the truck and asked him if Jim was one of the company's employees. The manager said he certainly was not, since his company was not in the habit of hiring known thieves.

Poor Jim was taken into custody before he had a chance to eat his breakfast. By the time the men arrived at the sheriff's office, the company's manager had called back to tell them the company office had been burglarized and the truck stolen. They cleared the case and recovered the stolen truck, although Trooper Page still wonders why Jim would be so stupid as to stop at a restaurant where three marked police cars were parked.

If at First You Don't Succeed . . .

Perseverance and determination are frequently the marks of successful people. But we emphasize *frequently,* meaning *not always.* Former Baltimore, Maryland, police officer Frank Walmer remembers a determined burglar who persevered until he managed to get himself arrested.

Walmer and his partner were dispatched to a burglary in progress in a residential neighborhood. "We arrived and contacted the woman who had called," Walmer said. "She told us that someone had been trying to break through her basement door and that he was still at it. As we stood in the living room, we could plainly hear all sorts of thumping and bumping coming from the basement."

The woman led the two officers down the stairs and showed them the door in question.

"It was just as she described," Walmer said. "Someone was on the other side of the door, methodically kicking

He twisted and wiggled and, with a great deal of effort, finally managed to squeeze through the hole he had made.

it in. The bottom panel was beginning to give way. In a moment or two a hand reached through, but the hole wasn't big enough yet."

More kicking gradually widened the hole while the officers looked on. When the opening was large enough, a head popped through.

"My partner and I were standing on either side of the door," Walmer says, "but the guy never looked around. He twisted and wiggled and, with a great deal of effort, finally managed to squeeze through the hole he had made. Breathing hard, he stood up, dusted himself off, and suddenly realized he was looking down two gun barrels.

"At that point," says Officer Walmer, "we felt we had a pretty strong case."

Mental Blocks 20

Responding to a burglary call in Birmingham, Alabama, Lieutenant Jay Macintosh arrived at the scene to find the would-be burglars lying, exhausted, in back of the building. Too tired to do anything but talk, they explained that they had come equipped with picks and sledgehammers to pound away at the thick brick wall.

When they finally broke through the bricks some forty-five minutes later, they were stunned at what they found. It seems that the building owners, in order to prevent flooding, had built up the back of the property and erected a retaining wall. It was this wall, not the wall of the actual store, that the burglars had worked so hard to breach. Once they were through, our stonebreakers found themselves not inside the building, but on the roof!

Ever heard the phrase "thick as a brick"? At any rate, these guys got some good practice for a future occupation: breaking rocks in a prison camp.

21 The (Ex)-Terminator

Sgt. Perry Knowles got a call one night announcing that shots were being fired at one of the juke joints in Pensacola, Florida. Knowles was only moments from the little tavern, so he responded immediately and sped to the scene.

A few moments after arriving, he realized he was the first on the scene and that the shots were still ringing out. They seemed to be coming from inside. Knowles drew his gun and cautiously approached the front door. Inside, people were still dancing and shooting pool as though nothing out of the ordinary was going on. Another shot rang out. Without waiting for backup, Knowles dashed in, just as another shot sounded from the back of the club.

Gun drawn, Knowles hurried down a hallway and then crept around the corner, where he saw a man facing the other way with a pistol in hand, following the path of a huge cockroach. *Blam!* He blasted the cockroach with a close-range shot from a .38 and blew a big hole in

Blam! He blasted the cockroach with a close-range shot from a
.38 and blew a big hole in the wall.

the wall. After two more direct hits, the (ex)terminator broke open his cylinder to reload. That's when Sergeant Knowles jumped out from behind the corner.

"What in the world are you doing?" Knowles yelled while disarming the man.

"Shooting cockroaches!" the shooter said, apparently seeing nothing odd about his answer.

"Why?" Knowles asked.

"Well, we've tried everything else, and nothing has worked."

In Your Face

Police captain Mike Coppage of Birmingham, Alabama, remembers the time that one of his fellow officers was on his way home in a marked unit and had just stopped by Shoney's, a restaurant known for its strawberry pies. He picked up a whole pie to go and was just about to leave the parking lot when a call came through from the dispatcher. A break-in had just occurred in a small business right behind the restaurant.

Leaving his patrol unit behind in the restaurant parking lot, the officer walked around to the crime scene and began his investigation. While he was dusting for prints, the officer suddenly heard a desperate cry for help on his walkie-talkie.

"Help! Help!" cried the voice. "I'm in trouble. Help me!"

The call was coming from a police radio. It was an officer in trouble!

In response, the police dispatcher desperately tried to

pinpoint the distressed officer's location: "Where are you? What is your location?"

"I don't know!" came the response. "Just send help."

"What is your patrol car number?" the dispatcher asked.

"I don't know."

Realizing now that it had to be a civilian on the police mike, and believing that the officer was too severely injured to respond, the dispatcher put out the call: "All units, officer down!"

"Sir," the dispatcher then said to the voice on the radio, "I need the number of the unit."

"Okay. I see it now. It's 412. Car 412."

By this time, our crime-scene officer was running back to his car at top speed when it dawned on him—car 412 was *his* unit. He raced back to his police cruiser, and there stood the man, still clutching the microphone. His face, neck, and the front of his shirt were covered with what had to be blood. He was breathing sporadically and obviously in a state of shock and confusion. The officer tried to calm the man down and was about to administer first aid when he noticed that the "blood" on his hands was thick and sticky. The man was covered with strawberry pie!

Wait a minute, thought the officer, *I just bought a . . . oh, man, don't tell me that. Noooo.* By now the cop was peering into his patrol car. It looked like an octopus had had a strawberry and whipped cream food fight in the backseat.

The "injured" man, a street person—and drunk out of his mind—had walked by and seen the pie in the cruiser's backseat. He had then crawled inside the squad car and helped himself to that strawberry pie without benefit of utensils. For some unknown reason, he had completely freaked out and called for help after eating the entire pie with his face.

"We laugh about it now," Captain Coppage says, "but at the time the officer was so mad he couldn't see straight."

Bedrock Blues

Sgt. Chip Simmons works undercover narcotics in a medium-sized city in the South. Like almost every other city in the United States, this particular city was known for having a few hot spots for drugs. The cops would do a sweep of those hot spots every few weeks or so, then the traffickers would get released and move a few blocks away to resume business. It was an ongoing cycle.

Sergeant Simmons was frustrated by this slow repetition of arrest, release, move on, and start up again. So he and his fellow officers would try to keep the trade in total chaos by staging frequent, sudden, and very visible "jump outs." Five or six plainclothes officers with badges and guns would target a hot spot for the evening, usually a nightclub parking lot, and, literally, jump out of an unmarked van to surprise the drug traffickers.

In the wee hours of a chilly morning, just about a half-hour before the legal closing time for taverns, Simmons and the van of officers eased in quietly to a space in a parking lot where twelve dealers were doing business. The dealers were already moving toward the van to sell dope to the new arrival when the back doors popped open and the Trojan van spewed out its load of narcotics officers. Dealers scattered, some falling to the pavement, some disappearing into the night, most finally surrendering.

Simmons collared one individual who was in possession of several "rocks" of crack cocaine but who didn't have any identification on him.

"What's your name?" Simmons asked.

"Tommy."

"Tommy what?"

"Tommy Smith, but most people call me Tiger."

"Tommy 'Tiger' Smith?"

"No, Thomas L. Smith."

The name games continued, and the officer got the distinct impression that this suspect was lying. Chip Simmons was the wrong man to choose for verbal sparring.

"Where do you live, Tiger?"

"Johnson Avenue," Tiger smugly replied.

"What number on Johnson Avenue?" Simmons asked, laying the bait.

"100 Johnson Avenue."

"The blue house?"

"Yeah, big blue house."

"And there's always a green car in the driveway?"

"That's my green car."

Simmons grinned from ear to ear. "Now I know you're lying."

Tiger was indignant. "I am not."

"I know you're lying, because I know who lives in that blue house. And it's not you; it's the Rubbles!"

Tiger's face went slack. He went back to rule number one of dumb crime: Deny, deny, deny!

"They do not!"

All the officers were now breaking into laughter as Simmons closed in for the kill.

"Yes, they do! Betty and Barney Rubble, good friends of mine, known 'em for years. They've always lived at 100 Johnson Avenue!"

Tiger was in a corner, but then a light went off in his empty little head.

"They don't live there now . . . because I bought the house from the Rubbles last month. That's who I bought the house from . . . the Rubbles! Betty and Barney!"

Later that night, Tiger's fingerprints revealed the dealer's real name. And guess what: it wasn't Fred Flintstone!

I Should Have Made That to Go

24

Sgt. Larry McDonald was called to a break-in at a Birmingham, Alabama, grade school one night. Upon arriving, he was met by another officer. While the backup unit staked out the front of the school, Officer McDonald walked around back and began looking through windows to see if the burglar might still be inside.

While walking past the cafeteria window, McDonald saw the intruder sitting at one of the lunchroom tables with a big hunk of ham in front of him. The burglar also had in front of him some mustard, bread, and a bag of potato chips. He was making himself a midnight snack. Problem was, it wasn't his food. Or his house.

"About the time I put my light on him, the officer in front had gained entrance to the school, so we placed the man under arrest and took him into custody," McDonald says. "He should have made that sandwich to go."

25 Debriefing

Bank robbing is one of those high-pressure profes-
sions. Stress certainly is part of the job—and one, we
presume, that is not covered in the group medical plan.

Not all bank robbers are up to the task. Take the case of
the Charlotte, North Carolina, bank robber, fleeing from
the scene of his crime. In a brilliant flash of inspiration,
he stripped to his underwear, figuring there was no way
he could be identified by specific articles of clothing.
Next, of course, he would stuff the large bundle of
heisted greenbacks down the front of his underwear.

His plan seemingly worked. No one came forward to
identify the robber. Someone, however, *did* call the police and point him out as the "sweaty man wearing nothing but strangely bulging underwear." The officers report
that after the man was "debriefed," the money was recovered.

This Guy Is Falling

26

Birmingham, Alabama, officer Ken McGinnis knows that there are times when serving an arrest warrant is anything but routine. There's always the chance that whoever is being arrested won't come without some show of force. But this was one arrest that made up for what it lacked in real danger with a few good belly laughs.

While serving the warrant, McGinnis and his partner stood at the door of the man's house and knocked several times, but no one answered, although they could hear movement inside. Finally, a woman answered the door and listened as the two officers explained why they were there. When they were finished, the woman said that she was the man's mother and hadn't seen her son in several days.

"Do you mind if we take a look inside, ma'am?" McGinnis asked.

"Not at all," she said. "Come on in and look around."

The two officers entered the house and started down the hallway with the mother right behind them. "Lord knows where that boy is," she was saying.

Then, abruptly, they heard a sharp cracking sound overhead, followed by a shower of plaster and a falling body. Their suspect hit the floor right in front of them. He did a belly flop and must have bounced two feet. Then he lay still, the wind knocked out of him.

After allowing the man time to catch his breath and brush off some of the plaster, McGinnis and his partner rolled the guy over and handcuffed him. "Guess the Lord *did* know where he was," McGinnis remembers. "And it was sure good of Him to pass along the information."

Unlucky Numbers

27

Officer Dennis Shepard was on routine patrol late one Friday night in the charming little town of Franklin, Tennessee, when he and his partner noticed a man scurrying along one of the main streets of town. The pedestrian appeared to be quite nervous and was clutching something in his hand while continually looking back over his shoulder. He also appeared to be trying to stay in the shadows, avoiding the street lamps.

As the officers' car approached him, the man's face lit up into a broad smile, and he began motioning frantically for them to pull over. Officer Shepard recognized him now. He was the man known locally as Pot Pie, a harmless individual who, over the years, had occasionally been arrested for public intoxication.

"Boy, am I glad to see you guys," Pot Pie blurted out. "I need a ride home, officers. This has been my lucky day!"

"Your lucky day?" they asked curiously. "How so?"

"I've been playin' the numbers for ten years, and today my ship came in. Looky here."

They looked at the bundle the man was waving in the air.

"What is it?" they asked.

"What it is," he said with pride, "is the seven hundred fifty dollars cash that I won today after all these years."

"You won this money gambling on the numbers?" the officer asked, hoping that it might dawn on Pot Pie what he was telling the police about his own illegal activity.

"I sure did," he answered with an even bigger grin. "Ten years, and I finally won. Seven hundred fifty dollars! Hot damn! I been out celebratin', and now I need a ride home to make sure nobody takes it away from me."

Shepard shook his head sadly. *Why didn't this guy just call a cab?* he thought. This was one of those times that he wished he didn't have to do what he was about to do.

"You sure you won that money playin' the numbers, Pot Pie?" he asked, still trying to find an out for the guy.

"Oh, yeah," he said. "I played the numbers all right, and here's the money to prove it."

The officers looked at each other. Pot Pie was as happy as could be. His grin reminded Shepard of one of those smiley-face buttons, and he hated being the one to paint on the big red circle with the slash through it.

"I'm afraid, then, that we're going to have to arrest you," he told Pot Pie.

"Arrest me? For what?"

"Don't you know that it's against the law to gamble on the numbers in Tennessee?"

"Sure, I do . . . but I won! I . . ." Then reality slowly set in. His face sank. "What about the money?" he asked.

"Well, I'm afraid we're going to have to confiscate the money as evidence."

Pot Pie's face sank even lower. "I was so happy winnin' that money that I plumb forgot that the numbers was against the law. Man, I should've called a cab!"

Actually, things didn't turn out so badly for our dumb criminal. When Pot Pie went to court, the judge took pity on him. He fined him court costs only and returned nearly five hundred dollars to him.

28 The Honeymoon's Over

Police officer Mary Wiley was used to working undercover. She had been involved in more than a hundred
prostitution stings in and around Birmingham, Alabama.
So she pretty much assumed she had seen it all—until
she met the man in the tuxedo.

When working a sting, Officer Wiley would pose as a
streetwalker while other officers monitored, from down
the street, her conversations with potential clients. Once
a deal was struck with a "john," or client, she would direct him to meet her around the corner, where he would
promptly be arrested for solicitation. If he was married,
the first question out of his mouth was likely to be, "Will
my wife find out about this?"

That's more or less what happened with the tuxedo-
clad gentleman. He pulled his car up to the curb, rolled
down the window, stuck his elegantly groomed head out
the window, and propositioned her. Wiley did her job,
and it wasn't until after the tuxedoed man had been

Believe it or not, the man had taken his wedding vows only four hours earlier.

arrested that she found out why he was dressed so nicely. It was his wedding day!

Believe it or not, the man had taken his wedding vows only four hours earlier. He'd left the reception, still dressed to the nines, to buy more beer, and he then apparently decided to stop for one more purchase.

"Is my wife going to find out?" he asked.

"I wouldn't worry too much about that," Wiley responded. "If she does find out, you probably won't have a wife anymore."

At the very least, we'd bet she threw a lot more than rice at him when he returned to the reception.

Yeah, and One Size Fits All!

29

Officer Max Kent was driving down the road on a balmy Florida evening, minding his own business, when a small car accelerated away from an intersection, spinning its tires for about twenty feet—"laying a patch," if you will.

Just another routine traffic stop, right? In this book? No way.

The small red car picked up speed as Kent hit his lights and siren. But almost as quickly as he floored it, the speeding driver began to brake and pull over. It would seem the driver had second thoughts about trying to run from the law.

Officer Kent approached the driver's side and began to question the man.

"Sir, could I see your driver's—"

Suddenly, the red car peeled out at full speed, spitting gravel and dust inches away from Kent's nose and toes.

The officer leaped back into his squad car and again gave chase as he called in for backup.

Again, the man pulled over within moments. This time Officer Kent drew his pistol as he approached the window.

The man was already waving his hands and screaming, "I'm sorry! I'm sorry! My foot slipped off the clutch, and I had the dang thing in gear."

Before Officer Kent got a chance to tell the gentleman what he thought of that story, the car scrubbed out one more time. This time Ol' Slippery Foot "slipped" down a residential side street that just happened to be a dead end. Officer Kent radioed in his position and jumped out of his car in a firing position. His gun was trained on the red car, now stopped in the cul-de-sac. He could just hear the man saying, "I'm sorry" again.

Then—you guessed it—his foot "slipped" once more. Only this time the red car was accelerating straight at Kent. He was ready to disable the vehicle or the driver or both when the car suddenly came to a halt about twenty feet away from Kent and his cruiser.

Needless to say, Kent got the suspect out of the car, cuffed him, and pulled him onto the pavement before his foot had another chance to "slip."

Gotta Match?

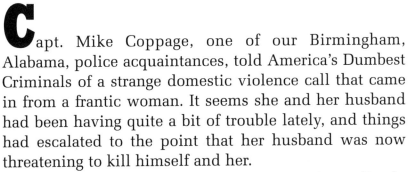

Capt. Mike Coppage, one of our Birmingham, Alabama, police acquaintances, told America's Dumbest Criminals of a strange domestic violence call that came in from a frantic woman. It seems she and her husband had been having quite a bit of trouble lately, and things had escalated to the point that her husband was now threatening to kill himself and her.

Police units and a S.W.A.T. team were immediately dispatched to the address, where they heard shouts and threats coming from inside the house. "I'll do it! Don't think I won't . . . 'cause I will. I'll kill myself!" Obviously, things were really getting out of control in there. When the police negotiator got the man on the phone, Coppage's crew realized just how bad it was.

"I'm gonna kill myself, the man threatened. "I've doused myself and the house with gasoline, and I'm gonna set myself on fire right now."

"Hey, we can work this out, Ronnie," the negotiator told him. "Come on outside. Let's talk about it."

"There ain't nothin' left to talk about, man. It's over."

Then the man set the phone down. There was an eerie silence.

Captain Coppage looked at the negotiator. He nodded his head. It was time to send in the S.W.A.T. team. The captain was about to give the signal to storm the house when suddenly the man was back on the line.

"Hey, y'all still there?" the man asked.

"Yeah, we're here."

"You got any matches?"

"Matches? You want matches?"

"Yeah, matches. You know, the kind you light? I can't find any in here."

"Let me look," the quick-thinking negotiator told him. "Yeah, I've got a book of 'em right here, Ronnie, but you're going to have to come out here and get them. I can't come in there."

"All right," Ronnie said. "I'll be right out."

True to his word, the man walked outside, where he was quickly apprehended.

Reach out and Touch Someone

Wanted for several dozen burglaries, East Coast fugitive Lester Willet had been eluding capture for several weeks. Although he had been seen in various bars, he always managed to be gone by the time the cops arrived. Friendly and outgoing, he had plenty of friends quick to tip him off each time the long arm of the law reached out to snag him.

But Lester Willet had a weakness, and her name was Charlene. A cocktail waitress at Taylor's Place, Charlene was a heavily made-up, gum-chewing, buxom beauty. Sadly, Willet's was an unrequited love, because Charlene adamantly refused to go out with him.

The investigator pursuing Willet learned about his infatuation with Charlene from one of his informants. He further learned that Charlene had this particular night off and that Willet had been calling her steadily from

Taylor's pay phone, trying to talk her into going out with him.

Seized by a sudden flash of inspiration, the investigator decided to have someone call Taylor's, impersonate Charlene's voice, and ask to speak to Willet. Once Willet got on the phone, it would be a simple matter to swoop down and capture him. It was a good idea, although finding a convincing female voice was going to be difficult. Then someone suggested Dan Bulger.

Bulger was a brash communications dispatcher who also happened to be a wonderful mimic. He was on duty at the time, so the investigator sought him out and explained the plan. The capture team would wait a block or so from Taylor's as Dan, using his best female voice, called the bar, identified himself as Charlene, and asked for Willet. When Willet picked up the phone, the team would be notified by one of the other dispatchers and then make their move.

Their scheme worked perfectly. The pay phone was close to the main door, and when the team came around the corner there was Willet, the phone jammed against one ear and his hand pressed against the other. "Baby, you know I'm crazy about you!" he yelled into the phone. "You go out with me and you won't regret it, I promise."

So intent was he on the conversation that he didn't

notice he was now surrounded by uniforms. He had a big smile on his face and was nodding his head. "Room nineteen at the Sunset Motel. Right."

The investigator stepped forward and tapped him on the shoulder. Willet looked up, and the smile disappeared. "Uh, I got to go, baby," he said. He hung up and shook his head. "Well, I hope you guys are happy. I was fixing to meet one of the finest-looking women I have ever seen, and she was even going to pay for the room."

It was just a short trip back to the jail, but Willet complained about his bad luck the whole way. Just to rub it in, the investigator had Dan come over from the radio room. Willet was being fingerprinted when Dan stepped to the door and, using his Charlene voice, said, "Honey, I told you to meet me at the Sunset Motel."

Willet spun around so fast he almost knocked over the fingerprint stand. Dan gave him a big smile. "But I've changed my mind, sugar. You pay for the room."

Color Me Dumb

Officers Robert Cox and Ed Leach of Birmingham, Alabama, were on patrol in an area known for its drug houses when they spotted five men, most of them familiar looking, in an old Datsun with expired tags. The car also had two different-colored fenders and was brown on one side and white on the other. The officers shook their heads over that eye-catching repair job while they issued the driver a ticket for the expired tags.

About three hours later, the police department received a call that a robbery had gone down at a convenience store. The getaway car was—you guessed it—a multicolored Datsun. Bingo! Because the driver's name was already known, officers knew where he lived. They proceeded straight to the house, where they arrested the driver and his four pals.

The suspects were stunned. They couldn't imagine how they had been caught so fast.

He Got a Charge out of It

33

The General Services Administration (GSA) has its own criminal investigators to handle reports of crimes in federal buildings. One afternoon they received a report that a man was attempting to steal an air conditioner from outside one of the federal buildings in Atlanta. GSA investigators hurried to the scene, but as it turned out they could have taken their time—because they were dealing with a dumb criminal.

This particular genius was using a huge meat cleaver to cut through the various hoses, pipes, and other lines connected to the air conditioner. The cleaver was metal. All metal. No wooden or plastic handles on this baby. It was 100 percent metallic, and it was doing a good job cutting the copper pipe and rubber hoses. Of course, air conditioners run on electricity, and the heavy cleaver did a good job of cutting the electrical lines as well. It also did a good job of conducting the electricity from the electrical lines into the would-be thief, who lit up like a Christmas tree.

When the GSA investigators arrived, they found the dazed and slightly singed suspect lying on the ground, his eyes still rolling around in his head. He offered no resistance, but he made it clear he wanted nothing more to do with that air conditioner.

The heavy cleaver did a good job of cutting the electrical lines as well.

How well do you know the dumb criminal mind?

When released from prison on May 7, 1980, Paul Geidel had spent more consecutive years in a U.S. prison than any other convict in U.S. history. He was seventeen when he walked in. How old was he when he walked out?

a) **60 years old.**
b) **77 years old.**
c) **85 years old.**
d) **93 years old.**
e) **101 years old.**

The answer is (c). Sentenced to prison for murder on September 5, 1911, Geidel walked out of the Fishkill Correctional Facility in Beacon, New York, a free man after having served sixty-eight years, eight months, and two days. He was eighty-five years old. Do you think his girlfriend waited for him?

On a Losing Streak

34

Back in those crazy days of the seventies, a college craze known as "streaking" was making the rounds in America. Thousands of students were trying their hand and baring their, well, everything on campuses, at public ceremonies, and in the parks and streets. Sure, it was just a college prank. But the community of Pensacola, Florida, had voted that any kind of public nakedness was offensive enough to merit being against the law, so police officers such as Sgt. Perry Knowles were charged with keeping the streakers off the streets.

Knowles and his partner were on a narcotics stakeout behind an old forties-style downtown hotel when they heard the call. A young man dressed in nothing but red shoes and a cowboy hat had chosen Main Street for an evening run.

Setting out to investigate the general area of the sighting, Knowles noticed something down an alley. A white object had appeared in a hedge about thirty feet down the alley. Knowles hit the spotlight and, with his partner, zeroed in on the Unidentified White Object. The officers didn't need binoculars to identify what it was. Sticking out of the bushes was a large, naked, human, well, posterior. And it was moving slightly, sort of bobbing up and down.

Knowles and his partner quietly walked up to the bobbing rump, noticing the red sneakers down below.

"What are you doing?" they asked.

Without looking up, the college kid tossed off a nonchalant reply, "Oh, I just streaked Main Street, and I can't find my clothes."

"Well, here, I've got a flashlight. Let us help you."

The kid thanked him, took the flashlight, and kept looking down for his shirt and pants and underwear. They found his clothes moments later, and Knowles gave him a ride downtown . . . completely dressed.

Out on a Limb

Birmingham, Alabama, police captain Mike Coppage tells of an unlucky criminal he came across after arriving on the scene at a two-story office building, responding to an attempted break-in. Coppage says "attempted break-in" because the man never got inside the building. In fact, he never actually got *onto* the building.

Captain Coppage walked around to the back of the property, shining his flashlight toward the rooftop. The roof was clear, but a man was standing in a tree right next to the building. Coppage recognized Toby, a well-known small-time thief.

"Toby," Coppage yelled, "get down from there!"

A shaky voice yodeled something back.

"What'd you say, Toby?" Coppage called again.

"I can't get down. I'm stuck," came the reply. He was talking like an amateur ventriloquist.

"You're stuck?"

"Yeah, if I fall from here I'll pull my foot off. Help me."

Coppage took a closer look. Toby had one foot stretched out and wedged tightly behind a drainpipe that ran up the side of the building. His other leg was wobbling on a medium-sized limb about twenty-five feet above the ground. "I don't know how he was managing to stay balanced on that limb," the officer remembers.

Police had to call for a hook-and-ladder truck to get him down. Toby was then arrested and taken to jail for attempted burglary and criminal trespass.

For all his ineptitude as a burglar, though, we think Toby showed great promise as a branch manager.

Mirror Image

Most wild-game poachers work at night in isolated areas. Unless they do something really stupid, odds are they won't get caught. Deputy Sheriff Ronald Saville of Fort Benton, Montana, remembers some elk poachers who would have escaped clean but for a bit of carelessness.

Acting on a tip that someone had been shooting elk in the area, the deputy and a state game warden checked the area. This being the middle of winter, they had no trouble following the blood trail across the snow to where the poachers had gutted the animal. But other than the gory elk remains, there didn't seem to be any useful evidence—until they examined the scene more closely.

There in a snowbank, where the poachers had backed up a truck to load the elk carcass, the officers found an imprint of a license plate. It took only a moment to obtain a registration. The dumb poachers were astonished when met by a law enforcement welcoming committee.

37 There Will Be an Additional Charge

One time while processing new prisoners at the downtown Birmingham, Alabama, jail, Capt. Arnetta Nunn was frisking a large woman for drugs and weapons when she touched what felt like a gun handle in the woman's girdle.

"What's that?" Nunn asked.

"That's a gun," the woman casually said. "But don't tell anybody I've got it."

"Don't tell anybody? Ma'am, I'm a police officer. I *have* to tell somebody."

Luckily, the woman was just dumb and not crazy.

"Are you right- or left-handed?" Nunn asked.

"I'm right-handed," the woman said.

"All right, then, with your left hand, reach into your girdle. Using your thumb and index finger, very slowly remove the gun from your pants."

In the next moment the officer was holding a fully loaded .38-caliber revolver. To go with the woman's original charges, she was charged with trying to smuggle a weapon into a correctional facility.

Captain Nunn recounts, " 'Don't tell anybody'? Why do I get all the fools?"

38 Do You Know Where Your Children Are?

Deputy Bill Cromie was patrolling the deserted streets of Phoenix, New York, around two in the morning when he noticed a fifteen-year-old boy pushing his bike along the street. Although it was unusual to see someone of that age out on the street at that time of morning, it was something else that drew Cromie's attention. Balanced on the kid's bike was a huge, glass-fronted china cabinet.

Cromie knew the boy. He pulled up beside him and asked the boy what he was doing with the china cabinet. Clearly nervous, the lad stumbled over his words but finally said he was taking the china cabinet home to his mother. Realizing how lame this story sounded, the kid eventually admitted he had stolen it from a house down the street.

"Those people have been away for a long time," he said, "and I didn't think they would miss it. Besides, my mom has always wanted one of these things."

The kid eventually admitted he had stolen it from a house down the street.

Because they were only a block from the boy's house, Cromie followed him home so Cromie could talk to his mother.

The mother answered the door, and Cromie explained he had apprehended her son with a stolen china cabinet. She in turn asked the boy why in the world he would break into that particular house. The kid gave his mother a surprised look. "Don't you remember, Mom? You told me to go get it."

Clearly flustered by his reply, she mumbled and stuttered for a minute, then finally used the same words her son had: "Well, they've been gone a long time, and I always wanted one of those china cabinets. I didn't think they'd miss it."

How Do You Spell "Police"?

39

Police officer Jerry Wiley was returning to the Birmingham, Alabama, station one evening after having successfully served a warrant on a suspected drug kingpin. Nine other officers were riding with Wiley in the police raid van. All wore solid-black fatigues with the word *Police* stenciled across them in *Sesame Street*-sized letters.

They were driving through a heavy drug-trafficking area when a guy on the corner started waving frantically at the vanload of cops, motioning for them to pull over to the curb.

"What's this guy want?" one of the officers asked.

"I don't know," Wiley responded. "Let's find out."

They pulled over to the curb, and the man walked up to Wiley's window. "Y'all wanna buy some rock?"

"Some rock what?" Wiley asked.

"Rock cocaine, man. I got somethin' really nice here. You gonna love it."

Almost on cue, Wiley and his nine fellow officers

looked at one another incredulously, took another look down at their clearly marked uniforms, then shook their heads in disbelief. Either this guy was illiterate, or he had smoked enough "coke" to suffer brain damage.

Wiley gathered his wits and, struggling to keep a straight face, asked, "Sure, man, whatcha got?"

"I got some twenty-dollar pieces here, man . . . real nice. How many you want?"

Wiley looked at the guys in back, nodded to them, and said, "Well, I guess I'd better take all of 'em."

That was their cue. The doors of the van burst open, and ten armed officers jumped out, shouting, "Police! Freeze! Get on the ground!"

Says Wiley, "You should have seen the look on that guy's face—it was one of sheer terror. I thought he was going to have a heart attack right there."

The intrepid drug salesman was arrested and charged with possession and sale of a controlled substance.

"Were it against the law to be stupid," Wiley says, "we could have charged him with that, too."

They Always Return to the Scene of the Crime

40

It's amazing how many people don't know when they're well off—like the man whom former Baltimore, Maryland, policeman Frank Walmer stopped for erratic driving.

"There was no doubt the guy was drunk," Walmer says. "But he came out of the car just crying his eyes out. He told me he had just been notified that his elderly mother, who had been in Provident Hospital for some time, was about to expire, and he was trying to get there in time to see her one last time."

Walmer asked the man if he had been drinking, and he admitted he had. "I didn't intend to be driving," the man said. "But when the hospital called, I didn't have no other way to get there."

Feeling compassion for the man, Walmer told him to park his car and offered to drive him to the hospital. Blubbering his appreciation, the driver did as he was

97

told. When the two men got to the hospital, the driver thanked Walmer effusively for his help, then dashed inside.

"I was glad to help him, but I have to admit I was a little suspicious," Walmer says. "There was just something about his behavior that didn't ring true."

Wondering if he was becoming too cynical, Walmer drove back to the man's automobile and parked a block away so he could keep an eye on it. Eight minutes later a cab containing the still-intoxicated driver arrived. Out he jumped, keys in hand, and headed for his car.

"I waited until he slid behind the wheel before I pulled in behind him and turned on my lights," Walmer says. "When I walked up to his car, he just shook his head and said, 'I knew this was going to be a bad day.' "

Why I Hate Family Disturbances

41

Most law enforcement officers hate family disturbance calls. Not only are they frustrating to handle, but there is also the real possibility that one or both of the combatants will turn on the interfering officer. Many law enforcement officers have been injured or killed while trying to calm down family fights.

Don Parker was a deputy with the Escambia County Sheriff's Department in Pensacola, Florida, when he handled a memorable family disturbance call. The address was a second-floor apartment in a two-story building. As Parker climbed the stairs and started down the outside walkway, he heard yelling and screaming from the end apartment. The door was standing open about four inches, and the hoarse tones of an obviously drunken male were being drowned out by the shrill soprano of an enraged female. Parker pounded on the door and identified himself. There was instant silence but no response, so he pounded again.

"At that point the door flew open and the drunk came charging through like a fullback running for daylight," Parker said. "Unfortunately, I had been a little careless, and instead of standing to one side I was standing directly in front of the door. The drunk charged straight into me, carrying me backward with his rush.

"I had only a brief impression of a very large man wearing blue checkered pajama bottoms and nothing else. He had wild, bloodshot eyes, shaggy hair, and two days' growth of beard. He was at least six inches taller than me and fifty pounds heavier. At the moment of collision, he grabbed me by the arms, pinning them to my side, and we shot across the walkway and crashed into the railing. The force of the assault bent me backward over the rail, and my straw Stetson spun away in the darkness."

The man was so strong that Parker was unable to move. "Put me in jail!" the man shouted. "Just put me in jail!"

"I tried to think of something I could say to quiet him," Parker says. "So I asked him, 'Why do you want to go to jail?' I asked as calmly as I could.

" 'Because I'm drunk!' he shouted, giving me a shake with each word, 'and I belong in jail!'

100

The drunk came charging through like a fullback running for daylight.

"Although I was still completely helpless, I looked him in the eye and said sternly, 'Okay, that's it. You're under arrest.' "

Immediately, a big smile lit up the drunk man's face.

" 'All riiiiight!' he said, releasing me abruptly. He turned and sprinted down the concrete walk, bare feet pounding, ran down the stairs, crossed the parking lot, opened the back door of my cruiser, jumped in, and slammed it behind him!"

By the time Parker got to his car there was nothing more for him to do. He holstered his gun and stood there breathing hard, trying to collect his shattered wits. After a moment the guy in the backseat yelled, "Hey, are we going to jail or what?"

Parker assured him he was indeed going to jail. The man settled back in the backseat and smiled, saying, "It's about damn time."

You Can Run, But . . .

42

Officer Jay Macintosh was a police sergeant at the time, pulling watch on the streets of Birmingham, Alabama, at four o'clock in the morning, when he pulled up next to a man at a traffic light. Because it was summertime, the guy had all the windows in his car rolled down. There was a light breeze and, when it shifted in Macintosh's direction, it carried the pungent, unmistakable smell of marijuana smoke.

The man then made a right turn on red, which is legal, but he didn't use his turn signal. Macintosh hit his lights, pulled the smoking dope over, and asked the guy to get out of his car and hand over his driver's license. He did.

Macintosh sniffed. The vehicle reeked of pot. "Do you have any objections to my searching your car?" Macintosh asked.

The only answer Macintosh got was the guy taking off running. Macintosh's instincts screamed, *chase him*, but he thought about it for a second and decided to stay put.

"I'm thinking, *I've got this guy's driver's license with his name, address, and picture on it. I know where he lives, and I've got his car, so where's he gonna go?*" Macintosh says. "I felt sorry for the guy, I really did. He seemed like a regular guy who was going through some rough times."

Macintosh was calling for a tow truck when he looked up to see that his runner had come back. "I'm sorry, officer," he told Macintosh. "I just panicked and took off. But I got about a block away and thought, *Wait a minute . . . the cop's got my driver's license and my car, and he's got me.*"

"I was right about him," Macintosh says. "He was a nice guy. He was going through a divorce, and he'd never been arrested in his life."

How 'bout Some Hot Wax with That?

43

It was a routine traffic stop, but Officer Grace Reid of Pensacola, Florida, knew that nothing is ever really routine when it comes to crime. There's always the possibility that the person you're stopping has a less-than-happy history with the law and might decide to do something crazy, so you have to be on your toes.

This particular gentleman seemed nervous from the moment Officer Reid saw him. He stepped from his car and started eating something from his pocket. Either the guy was eating a powdered substance such as cocaine, or he had stashed some powdered-sugar doughnuts for a snack and had decided just to eat the sugar.

Reid grabbed the guy, spun him around, and cuffed him quickly, then spun him back and tried to get whatever it was out of his mouth. If it was what she thought it was and he managed to ingest too much of it, he would probably overdose and she wouldn't have a case.

As she went for his mouth, he went for his coat pocket with his now-cuffed hands. He tossed some more cocaine onto the trunk of Reid's cruiser and spun around, smashing his face onto her trunk in an attempt to scarf down four plastic packets of powder. Reid kept pulling him up, and he kept going back to lick her trunk.

Reid finally got him into the backseat of the cruiser and retrieved enough evidence to arrest and convict him. It was not the first time she had seen a suspect try to eat the evidence, but it was definitely the first time she had had a suspect wash her squad car with his tongue.

Merry-Go-Round

44

It was a cool April evening in the Florida Panhandle when Officer Tony Jordan spotted a couple in a pickup veering all over the road. The gentleman at the wheel would slowly fade over into the oncoming lane and then suddenly jerk back into his lane.

Officer Jordan caught up with them and signaled for them to pull over. With some difficulty, they pulled into the parking lot of a shopping center. As Jordan walked toward the vehicle, Jordan could hear the couple arguing.

After the man stepped from the car, Jordan asked the driver's wife, who also seemed intoxicated and a bit peeved, to stay put and not to start or move the vehicle. Jordan administered the field sobriety test to the man, who failed miserably. The man pleaded with the officer not to arrest him and insisted that his wife had had less to drink and was therefore capable of driving them both home.

Sure enough, as he spoke the words, the guy's wife

fired up that old truck and started to pull away, slowly. The officer cuffed the man and told him not to move, then jumped into his squad car to follow her. With lights flashing and siren sounding, he pursued the woman who was just a few car lengths ahead of him and barely moving.

"Stop the truck, ma'am, and turn off the key!" Jordan bellowed over his loudspeaker. But the woman just kept fleeing at ten miles per hour.

"Ma'am, please stop the truck!" Jordan yelled repeatedly, in between calls for backup. "Stop the truck and turn off the key!"

By this time Jordan was getting nauseous. After about ten minutes of this grueling, extremely low-speed chase in circles, the woman veered toward the mall and almost struck a building. Three other cruisers closed in and surrounded the fleeing motorist. When they opened the door to the pickup, the woman fell out and had to be supported. The loops mixed with the alcohol had gotten to her, too.

When it was all over, Officer Jordan and both his suspects took a slow, straight drive to the jail.

A Fool and His Tools Are Soon Parted

45

Lt. Jay Macintosh of Birmingham, Alabama, was working at the East Precinct at the time. He had just received a call from one of the officers at the North Precinct asking if Macintosh was familiar with a guy named Troy, a local burglar. Macintosh said yes, he had arrested Troy in the past. Well, this time it seems there had just been a break-in at a Sears store, and Troy's wallet had been found at the scene.

"I knew where Troy lived," Macintosh says, "so I went over to his house to see if he was around. I'd just pulled up and turned off my lights when here comes Troy down the street in his car. When he gets closer, he sees me sitting there and slows down. Then he just stops his car.

"I get out of my squad car, walk up to his window, and say, 'Troy, let me see your driver's license, please.' "

Troy began feeling around in his back pockets and then

started patting his shirt pockets and looking around on the seat. "I can't find my wallet, officer," he said.

"I didn't think you would," Macintosh said.

"You didn't?"

"Nope. I didn't."

Macintosh began to shine his light into the backseat of Troy's car. It was loaded with new power tools.

"Hey, Troy, let me ask you something, man. You got a sander I could borrow?"

Old Troy just hung his head. He stepped out of the car and put his wrists together.

"By the way," Macintosh told him, "we've got your wallet down at the station."

The Kickstand Caper

46

Dennis Larsen was a motorcycle cop in Las Vegas in the seventies when he ran into a unique law enforcement situation.

Larsen was making a routine traffic stop in Vegas at about ten o'clock one night. He pulled over a speeding pickup and parked his motorcycle on the side of the road with the kickstand down on the semi-soft shoulder. Officer Larsen was at the driver's-side window of the pickup asking for the man's driver's license and registration when he heard the horrible, unmistakable sound of a heavy, well-equipped police motorcycle crashing to the pavement. His kickstand had broken.

Now, police motorcycles are not your little, lightweight dirt bikes. They are big, heavy machines. Larsen asked the speeding motorist to help him get his bike up off the shoulder of the road. Then Larsen hopped on and began to make a beeline for the police garage.

On the way to the garage, unfortunately, he spotted a

little street bike zipping in and out of lanes, cutting people off, and generally being extremely reckless. There was no way Larsen could stop anyone without an operational kickstand on his bike, but the guy driving the street bike was being a real jerk.

Finally, Larsen flipped on his lights and siren and gave chase. The biker pulled over in the next block. Larsen pulled over behind him. Larsen, still sitting on his bike, raised one hand and motioned for the man to come over to his bike. "I want you to straddle the front tire of my bike and grab my handlebars with both hands," Larsen said.

The man looked puzzled but did as he was told. Then Larsen finally was able to let go of his bike and step off. He asked for the man's license, and the gentleman explained it was in his wallet in his back pocket. Larsen retrieved the wallet and the license, while the man kept a firm grip on the handlebars. Larsen then began writing the ticket.

After the paperwork was done, he placed his ticket book on his bike's front bumper and again took the handlebars.

"Now, please sign the ticket, sir," Larsen said.

The man let go of the handlebars and signed his ticket.

"Now, please put your hands back on the handlebars, sir."

The man did exactly as he was told and grabbed the bike again. Larsen tore off the man's copy of the ticket and stuffed it in the guy's shirt pocket. He then took the handlebars back from the biker and hopped onto his bike.

"You know," the man said, "I've been stopped before, but nobody has ever made me stand like that and grab the handlebars. Is that some new thing the cops do now?"

"No, sir. My kickstand broke about ten minutes ago, and I was on my way to the police garage to get it fixed."

The man scratched his head again. "So, what would you have done if I hadn't stopped?"

"All I would have been able to do was radio it in and follow you until I ran out of gas."

"What would you have done if I had dropped your bike and made a run for it?"

"Well, my bike weighs too much for me to pick it up and chase you, so I couldn't have followed you."

DUMB CRIMINAL QUIZ NO. 417

How well do you know the dumb criminal mind?

With such illicit drugs as cocaine, crystal "meth," and even heroin so prevalent in our society, a recent study was done in Los Angeles to determine what percentage, if any, of the paper money in circulation might be tainted with traces of these drugs. (Bills collect residue when they are rolled up and used as straws to snort the drugs.) What percentage did the study reveal?

a) 3 percent
b) 75 percent
c) 51 percent
d) 18 percent
e) 0 percent

The answer is (b). A whopping 75 percent of all paper money tested in Los Angeles contained trace amounts of these drugs!

It's Later than You Think

47

Detective Jerry Wiley of Birmingham, Alabama, offers this story of stupidity concerning a man who entered a convenience store and told the young female cashier to back away from the register.

"Don't hit that button under there, either," he told her.

"How do you know what that button is?" she asked.

"Honey, I've been robbin' these here little stores since before you were born, that's how I know. I robbed my first one at the tender age of eleven."

The man took the money from the drawer, casually counted it, and stuffed it into his pocket. He then winked at the young girl as he opened the door to leave and said, "You'd have to get up pretty early in the morning to catch old Bo Ramsey!"

When the police arrived, the cashier described the man and repeated what he had said. They ran his name through the computer and got a copy of his driver's license, with picture I.D., which they showed the clerk.

"Yep, that's him. That's the pro."

48 Dumber Indemnity

Having just received an eviction notice from his landlady for nonpayment of rent, Henry came up with a brilliant idea that would allow him to, one, get revenge on his landlady and, two, grab some real cash! All he needed was a renter's insurance policy and a couple of cans of gas.

Henry bought an insurance policy with a benefit of ten thousand dollars. He then informed all his Pensacola, Florida, neighbors that he had to take a short trip out of town and would be back in a couple of days. No one would ever suspect!

He returned after dark, parked his car around the block, took two five-gallon gasoline cans from his trunk, and made his way stealthily through a wooded lot behind the house. Creeping to an open window, he poured in the ten gallons of gasoline. All he had to do now was let the gasoline soak in a bit, throw a match through the window, and saunter back to his car.

All he had to do now was let the gasoline soak in a bit.

Unfortunately, gasoline does more than soak in; it fills any space with explosive fumes very quickly. Henry threw the match through the window and gave new meaning to the term "shotgun shack."

Brushing pieces of the house off himself, Henry limped to his car. Meanwhile, a quick-thinking neighbor who saw him had called 911. A patrolman, hearing the dispatcher's description of the car, quickly spotted Henry and pulled him over.

When the patrolman asked Henry to step out of his car, he was overpowered by the smell of pine. "Someone just set my house on fire, and I'm trying to catch him!" Henry told the officer. The officer, shining his flashlight into Henry's car, saw a can of pine air freshener on the seat.

"I see," the officer said. "What kind of car was he driving?"

As Henry continued his story, unfortunately, his pine cologne began to fade, giving way to the distinctive odor of gasoline.

On what must have been a long ride to the station, he asked the patrolman, "Do you think they'll still pay on my insurance policy?"

Dumber than That Even

Detective Buddy Tidwell, now of Nashville, Tennessee, started out his career on the small police force of a quiet rural community.

One evening Buddy got a call from a neighbor describing one of the most unusual thefts in county history. It seems that Mr. McDonald had dropped off a truckload of hay about eighty miles away in the next county. Coming back, his truck had started to overheat, so McDonald had pulled over near a stream to give the forty-year-old Ford a cool drink from the creek. That's when three joyriding punks pulled up and decided to give Ol' McDonald a rough time.

"Hey, ol' man, nice ride," they hooted. "You must be one of them rich farmers with a million bucks stuffed in his mattress in an old sock, right?"

McDonald just shook his head and muttered under his breath, but he wasn't really in a position to fight off the three of them. So the punks took the old man's wallet and ran.

Going through the wallet, the punks discovered not only McDonald's hay money, but also the receipts for a VCR and a big-screen TV he had just purchased. The thugs decided to call the phone number they had also found in the wallet. McDonald answered. The punks said they knew where he lived and that they wanted his new TV and VCR. If McDonald didn't put all the new merchandise into a box on the lawn before nine that night, they said, they would come in and get him and his wife. The old farmer finally called the police. Buddy Tidwell took the call.

"The old guy was pretty scared, so we told him to get his family out of there and down to the station immediately," Tidwell says. "Then we rolled."

When the officers got to the house, they hid their cars. Buddy found the empty boxes for the TV and VCR still sitting in the garage. His partner helped him fill up the boxes with the first thing they could find in the garage—paving stones, lots of 'em. They quickly duct-taped the boxes up and slid them onto the lawn in front of the house. Then they took up positions in the bushes and waited.

Right on schedule, the punks pulled up, driving slowly with their headlights turned off. The three youths got out of the car, then tried to lift the biggest box of rocks.

"It probably weighed two hundred fifty pounds," Tidwell says, "but these boys managed to get it up and started to run, well, walk real fast with it."

The officers let the punks get pretty far along before they called out and identified themselves. They called for the fleeing thieves to stop, but the fools wouldn't. Instead, they changed direction and tried to jog into the woods with their heavy loot.

"We just kind of jogged behind them," Tidwell says. "We never got too close because we wanted them to carry that box as far as they could."

The criminals finally just wore out and collapsed, giving themselves up to Buddy and his partner. The officers couldn't wait to show them just what they had risked their lives to drag through the woods.

"At that point," remembers Buddy, "they definitely felt dumber than a box of rocks."

50 Should Have Stayed in Seventh Grade

A man presented himself to Sgt. Thomas Pennington at Las Vegas, Nevada, police headquarters to inquire as to why a narcotics detective had been looking for him. There was a one-million-dollar, drug-trafficking charge outstanding on the man in California, but he assumed he couldn't be arrested for it in another state. The desk sergeant explained the law to him as he snapped on the cuffs.

The One-Armed Orangutan

51

The ownership of exotic pets often seems to lead to frantic calls of one sort or another to police. One began as a routine burglary call. When Officer Ronnie Allen of Oklahoma City, Oklahoma, arrived at the apartment, he was greeted by an elderly gentleman. Senior citizens are all too often easy prey for burglars and other criminals, so Allen was feeling bad for the guy while he began the routine process of listing the stolen items. Then the old gent made a startling statement.

"But what I'm really worried about is my one-armed orangutan. He can get downright nasty when he's not fed."

"Your what, sir?"

"My one-armed orangutan. He's only about four-foot-six, but apes are unusually strong for their size, especially a one-armed ape. His left arm is as strong as three men's arms."

"You had a one-armed orangutan here?"

"Till he got stolen or ran off. He was here when I left. One of these burgers was for him. He'll be angry that he didn't get his burger."

At this point, Allen didn't know if the old guy was confused, pulling his leg, or the genuine owner of a missing one-armed orangutan. It's not something you want to call in without being really sure of what you're saying. But the old guy's story was confirmed when Allen heard a disturbance call from an apartment nearby. It seems a group of larcenous individuals were sitting around taking inventory of the items they had just stolen from the old man's apartment. The burglars were also inhaling toxic paint fumes to "cop a cheap buzz."

Unfortunately for them, the cracked crooks had forced a certain one-armed orangutan, who just happened to be hanging out with them, to sniff the paint, too. The drugged-out ape had gone berserk and was wreaking havoc in the apartment. The police had to get the old man to talk the orangutan out so that the burglars could give themselves up to police without being torn apart.

The Long Windshield of the Law

52

Veteran officer Johnny Cooley of Birmingham, Alabama, had been patrolling the same stretch of interstate highway for twenty-four years. He had seen it all on this one small portion of superslab. As with a lot of the officers we've interviewed, though, no stories sprang immediately to his mind. So we took a little ride with him.

As he drove us down the otherwise unremarkable stretch of highway, memories and stories started flooding back with each mile marker we passed. When we passed the one marked "38," he suddenly started to laugh . . . and we mean belly laughs, the kind that bring tears to your eyes. This is the story he told of the bust at mile marker 38.

The officer was actually off duty and was just headed home in the right-hand lane of a four-lane highway. His radar gun was off, he was off the clock, and as far as he was concerned he was just another guy driving home from work. He was, however, the only guy on the highway driving a police cruiser home.

Out of the corner of his eye, he noticed a car swerving erratically and then speeding up in the left lane. The officer watched as the car kept accelerating, veering in and out of lanes, narrowly missing several cars. The four men in the car, obviously, had either done something wrong or they were intoxicated . . . or both. So the officer called in the incident on his radio and fell in behind the speeding car with his lights lit and the siren screaming.

The guys in the car sped up. They shot in between cars, veered out onto the shoulder, and darted back up onto the road, trying to lose the trailing cop. Eventually, the officer noticed that the two men in the backseat were tossing something out the windows. An object hit the police cruiser's windshield as other items flew past the squad car. Then, suddenly, the fleeing car pulled over, right by mile marker 38.

The officer cautiously approached the car and asked the occupants to step out. The four men complied willingly, coyly acting as though they had no idea why the officer had stopped them.

"What was that stuff you guys were throwing out the window?"

The officer knew it had to be drugs, but there were no drugs in the car, and none of the men had drugs on his person.

126

An object hit the police cruiser's windshield as other items flew past the squad car.

"Aw, that was just a cigarette pack," one lousy liar said while grinning really big. "I'm sorry. I guess you got me for littering." The other passengers laughed.

As his backup arrived, the officer took the four men's licenses back to his squad car to run a check for prior arrests or any outstanding warrants. That's when he noticed the object lodged on the windshield wiper of his squad car. Reaching over, he plucked off an overstuffed bag of marijuana.

The dopers had scored a direct hit, but it was the officer who hit the jackpot. He had collared four of the biggest dealers in the city. No one was laughing now—except for the officer, of course.

Calling All Cops

53

Beepers can be a disadvantage for dumb crooks in more ways than one. Such was the experience of an undercover narcotics officer in Florida nurturing a relationship with a known drug dealer who was a first-class slimeball and a major source of crack cocaine.

Making a narcotics buy without entrapment and with as much admissible evidence as possible is the goal of every undercover narcotics investigation. This particular officer had socialized; that is, he had seen and been seen in all the right places by his target. Gradually, over a two-month period, he had developed a relationship with the dealer. Finally, the officer had made his first buy, and he and the dealer had exchanged pager numbers so they could arrange future transactions.

The stage was set for a second buy. If this operation was done properly, the cops would then have cash, drugs, audio recordings, still photographs, and video on this guy—hopefully enough to convict him of drug trafficking and put him away.

But then the suspect made an interesting mistake. He called the undercover officer's pager to alert his "customer" that the stuff was in and the deal was going down, but he got the last number of the officer's beeper number wrong. The number he accidentally dialed just happened to be the pager number for the police department's S.W.A.T. team. Eighteen heavily armed, highly trained, sharpshooting officers answer that number.

Luckily, our undercover officer was also a member of the S.W.A.T. team, so he got the beep. And like all of the other seventeen S.W.A.T. team members, he answered the page by calling the number that appeared on his pager. Only when he recognized the answering voice as his dealer did the officer figure out what was going on. He quickly switched into his undercover persona.

"Hey, man, is it going down?"

By now the dealer was totally confused and totally paranoid, because by now he had already talked to about five officers who were answering the S.W.A.T. team page by calling the dealer's home number from the page and identifying themselves. Every cop in town seemed to be calling his number, and he had no idea why.

"Who is this?" he demanded of the undercover officer.

"It's me, Jimmy T.," the narcotics officer said, giving his drug-buying pseudonym.

"Man, I beeped you about ten minutes ago, and then the cops started calling. I ain't kidding, man. Five cops have called here in the last five minutes!"

Now the officer was scrambling to fix any possible damage. Luckily, he had himself a bona fide dumb criminal. "Wait, what number did you call?" he asked.

The dealer told him, and he laughed. "You got the last number wrong. My pager number ends in seven, not eight. You must've called the cops!"

"I must have."

"Did you say anything?" the officer said, fearing his cover had been blown and fishing for information.

"No! I just told them that it must've been a wrong number."

"Whoa, dude. Close call. So, do you have the stuff?"

The dealer and the undercover officer met within the hour, and as they did their business they both laughed about the erroneous beep. Their laughter was captured on audio and videotape along with the deal that convicted the dealer.

The Bare Facts

Working radar on a blistering summer's day is not the job assignment of choice for most law enforcement officers. It was just such a day that Officer Bill Cromie was running radar in a small town in upstate New York.

"I was sitting right by the side of the road with my air conditioning running, letting the sight of my marked car slow the speeding drivers and actually blinking my headlights at some of the faster ones," Cromie says.

So far he had been able to avoid having to actually write a single ticket. But he could see off in the distance a car approaching at a high rate of speed. Cromie blinked his headlights, but the vehicle didn't slow.

Cromie set off in pursuit. By the time he caught up to the speeder, she was still doing over fifty miles per hour. When she saw his blue lights, she pulled over. Cromie got out of his car, ticket book in hand, and then did a double take.

"Looking through the rear window I could see she was alone in the car, but she seemed to be shrinking. With each step that I took, she slid that much lower in the front seat. I was about to ask for her driver's license, but I only got as far as, 'May I see your—' because I suddenly realized I could see her—*all* of her. The woman was stark naked."

At that point it was hard to say who was more embarrassed and, blushing furiously, Cromie turned his back on the cringing woman. "I suppose I was taking a risk, but I was fairly sure she wasn't carrying any concealed weapons. Of course, I asked her how it was that she came to be driving her car, naked, at a high rate of speed."

The woman told him that she had been driving beside a river, and it had looked so cool and inviting that she just had to take a quick swim. Picking what she thought was a deserted section, she had peeled off her sweaty clothing and dived in. The water had been wonderful, but as she floated with the current she had seen two fishermen emerge from bushes and sit on the bank only a few feet from where she had left her clothes. Intent on catching fish, they hadn't seen her or her clothes, but they obviously had posed a major problem for the swimmer.

From the looks of things, they had settled in for the day.

Luckily, the woman's keys were still in the car, so she had swum around a bend in the river and waded ashore, creeping past the unsuspecting fishermen. She had been able to get to her car undetected and was headed for home when Cromie stopped her.

Convinced she had to be telling the truth, he said he would let her go without writing her a ticket. The woman expressed her gratitude, but wanted to know if Cromie had a coat she could borrow. He didn't. Unhappy with his answer, she insisted that he help her.

"I told her the only thing I could give her was my uniform, but that would have been pretty hard to explain if she got stopped again. She finally drove off, still hunkered down in the seat. But at least she was doing the speed limit."

Fooled You

55

Police captain Arnetta Nunn of Birmingham, Alabama, is a real charmer, so much so that one dumb criminal actually sought her out.

Nunn was working in plain clothes and driving an unmarked car at the time. She had just walked out of city hall and crossed the street to her car when a man approached her from behind.

"You want to buy some rings?" he asked Nunn. "I stole these in Tennessee."

"You stole them?" Nunn asked.

"Yeah, up in Tennessee, and I really need some money right now, so I'm sellin' 'em real cheap. This stuff is top of the line."

Well, Nunn took a look at some of the rings and found them to be cheapo stuff with high-dollar tags.

"I picked up one ring and kind of held it up to my eye," Nunn remembers, "and he says, 'Don't let the man see you!' He was nervous and kept looking around, and then he looked down into the front seat of the car and saw the police radio on the floorboard."

At this point the man asked Nunn if she was with the police. She answered in the affirmative.

"You ain't got nothin' on me," he said self-assuredly. "This stuff ain't stolen, and I can prove it. So, ha! You can't touch me. You're a fool, lady."

That made Nunn mad, especially the "fool" part. Here's some two-bit con man out here on the streets scamming people's hard-earned money from them and telling Nunn there was nothing she could do about it. She was determined to prove him wrong.

"You want to walk over to city hall with me and find out who the real fool is?" Nunn asked him.

"Sure, I'll go over there with you. I told you, you can't touch me."

Nunn and her newfound acquaintance walked across the street. Every step of the way, Nunn was thinking, *What can I nail this guy on? If he can prove those rings are really his, then there goes that charge.* They walked into city hall, where Nunn told him to just have a seat and she'd be right back to book him.

Just then a veteran of twenty years walked up and asked Nunn what she had out in the hall. She explained the situation to him, and he casually said, "There's a city ordinance that prohibits the sale of merchandise on the street within a six-block radius of the downtown loop without a license. Does he have one?"

Holding back a chuckle, Nunn walked back out into the hallway and said to the man, "Do you have a license to sell that junk in the loop area?"

Stunned silence.

"I didn't think so. Follow me, please."

"Follow you where?" he asked with a puzzled look.

"Back to the booking room. You're under arrest for failure to procure a city license to sell in the loop area. C'mon, fool."

56 What's in a Name?

Retired FBI agent Fred McFaul remembers when he was a young and newly assigned agent in Florida. A veteran agent had been working a bomb threat extortion case and asked Fred to come along while he interviewed the suspect. The case involved an unknown person who had been demanding money from a local business and threatening to blow up the business if the demands were not met. The suspect was a man named Robert Moore.

"We drove to the suspect's house, located in a small town in northwest Florida," McFaul says. "The guy was quite willing to talk with us."

The two agents had a long and rambling conversation with Robert Moore, but made no real headway. He continued to deny that he had anything to do with the bomb threats. Also, they were having a bit of a communication problem.

"I was from the North," McFaul says, "and I had a little trouble understanding the suspect's southern accent.

Every so often, I would have to ask him to repeat something."

Our suspect was in the process of telling the two agents how innocent he was, when he again said something that McFaul did not catch. "It sounded like he said, 'All these people, they be saying that Bomb Moore been making them threats, but it ain't true.' Now, I knew his name was Robert, and I thought he must have said *Bob,* but it really did sound like *Bomb.* I asked him to repeat the name he had called himself, and his eyes suddenly got real big."

The suspect hemmed and hawed for a few minutes. Finally, he admitted that the word was indeed *Bomb,* but that it was only a nickname.

"I asked him how he came to have such an explosive nickname," McFaul says, "and by then he was starting to sweat. A little more prodding, and he admitted he had been given the name because as a young man he liked to 'blow things up.' "

After that, it didn't take the agents long to obtain a full and complete confession.

57 Fail Safe

It was after midnight in Illinois when two thieves finally made it to the second floor of an old office building. It had taken them more than an hour to cut a hole in the roof big enough for the two very large men to squeeze through.

It was a hot summer night, and they were already sweating profusely by the time they found the three-hundred-pound safe in the manager's office. Within minutes, one was cutting around the door frame with an acetylene torch while the other was attempting to knock the tumbler off the safe with a sledgehammer. After forty-five minutes they were exhausted. They couldn't get it open.

"I've got an idea," one of them said. "Let's take it over to the window and drop it into the alley. With all the damage we've done to it, it should bust wide open when it hits!"

After pouring some water from the office cooler on the

"With all the damage we've done to it, it should bust wide open when it hits!"

safe to cool it down, they dragged, pushed, and lifted the steaming safe up to an open window and shoved it out.

The safe landed below with a tremendous crash and clanging sound as it hit the garbage cans. The men quickly ducked down as if they were two little kids who had just beaned somebody with a water balloon. After a moment or two they peeked out. Apparently, nobody had heard.

The two persistent thieves huffed downstairs and broke out through a back door. They hurried down the alley, jumped into their pickup, and pulled up next to the safe. With their adrenaline still pumping hard, they managed to hoist the hot safe into the back of the truck. Then they drove it out of town about twenty miles until they came to a railroad crossing.

"It's 2:20 now," one of them said to the other. "In about ten minutes the CSX [train] out of Decatur is gonna come roaring by here at about sixty miles an hour. So we put the safe on the tracks, the train hits it, and, *pow*, it busts wide open. The engineer will never know he hit anything."

"You're a genius, man," his friend acknowledged.

So with some more huffing and puffing the two brainiacs managed to wrestle the safe out of the truck and onto the railroad tracks. And not a moment too soon.

"Here she comes!" the first man announced. Both of

them hurried off the tracks and ran to duck behind the truck.

It happened just like the crook had predicted. The train's engineer never knew he'd hit anything. He didn't slow down a notch. The speeding train struck the safe at sixty miles per hour just as planned. But instead of bursting open and being tossed aside, the safe caught on the front of the train and was carried off down the tracks into the night. The two men stared in silent disbelief at the fading caboose light. They looked at each other. Neither one spoke. They got into the truck and went home.

But the story was not yet over. Unbeknownst to the two men, a woman had heard the two thieves as they were loading the safe into the back of the truck in the alley. She had taken down their license number and phoned the police, who showed up the following day to arrest them. The safe was found at a switching yard in the next town.

58 I Was Only Trying to Help . . . Myself

Officer Ernest Burt was once called to a break-in at a jewelry store in Birmingham, Alabama, during, appropriately, a terrible ice storm. Because few people were able to get around that night, the thieves figured the police wouldn't be able to, either. Wrong.

When Burt et al arrived at the scene, they saw that the front window had been knocked out of the store. Several people could be seen walking around inside the place. Burt and his fellow officers entered the store through the broken window and promptly arrested the six people inside.

"We had gone back into the store to try and find something with which to block up the window, when one of the officers turned to me and said, 'There's still somebody in here,'" Burt says. "I've been a police officer long enough to know that when another cop gets that feeling in his stomach, you pay attention to it. So we looked

144

around some more and, sure enough, we found two more intruders. Then we found another one hiding in the back. That brought the grand total to nine. You've got to listen to those gut feelings."

All nine men arrested were carrying jewelry and watches in their pockets, and yet they still denied being in there to rob the place. Every one of them said he had just gone in to stop the others from taking anything and that he was only trying to help. Right.

"We heard them arguing among themselves later and discovered that the lookout man had gotten cold and gone inside to warm up," Burt says. Then he laughs, "We put them all on ice."

59 I Dare You

Ah, spring, when young people's minds turn to thoughts of Spring Fest. The first warm days bring out thousands of college students eager to celebrate the end of winter. Oswego County (New York) Deputy Sheriff Bill Cromie remembers one particular Spring Fest that had all the required ingredients: a beautiful day, ten thousand thirsty college students, and a few hundred kegs of beer.

Although Cromie was off duty that day, he and the rest of the department were called in to back up the shift deputies trying to deal with a near riot caused by too many young people and too much alcohol at one site. By the time Cromie arrived, the celebration had been halted and the drunken celebrants told to disperse.

A bus company had been hired to transport the kids, and the deputies were allowing the buses to enter the party area one at a time to pick up their loads of passengers. One at a time the buses would travel down the single road, fill up with students, then return along the same road while deputies held up the traffic to allow them to pass.

"The kids were still yelling and shouting and screaming and laughing," Cromie says, "and most of the poor bus drivers looked about done in. But then another bus approached, and the bus driver actually looked happy. I was surprised, because this bus seemed to have the wildest bunch of all. They were hanging out of every window, screaming their heads off, and pounding on the sides of the vehicle. Still, I got a good look at the driver, and there he was with a big smile on his face. I remember thinking that at least here was one guy who was enjoying himself. I also noticed the number on the bus as it passed us. It was 105."

Cromie and his buddies continued to direct traffic, and a short while later a man approached him on foot. "I saw he was wearing a shirt and tie, which was unusual, and that he didn't look too happy. He said that he was a bus driver, but his bus was missing, and he thought some of the college kids had stolen it. I asked him what the number was. It was 105."

It took Deputy Cromie only a moment to radio ahead, and within five minutes the hijacked bus had been stopped. Because Cromie was the only one who had gotten a good look at the driver, he had to identify him.

"Of course, it was one of the students, and he was

147

drunk as a skunk. He told me the other kids had offered him five bucks each to take the bus, and they had dared him as well."

The temptation had been irresistible, and when a hat full of money was dropped into his lap, the student had succumbed. Now filled with remorse, he apologized for taking the bus and offered to give all the money to the bus driver if he wouldn't press charges. Cromie said it was too late for that and, besides, there was the small matter of the D.U.I. charge.

As the kid was being handcuffed, he tried to explain his actions one more time. "But you don't understand," he wailed. "They dared me to do it!"

Dogged
Determination

Sgt. Doug Baldwin of Pensacola's (Florida) finest was working narcotics one hot summer day when he observed a man in a blue Camaro making a drug buy. While other officers closed in on the dealer, Baldwin chased the customer. The customer, unable to lose the officer in his Camaro, jumped from his car and scampered away on foot with Baldwin in pursuit.

Baldwin watched as the man scaled a tall chain-link fence and crept under a car parked within the fenced compound. He kept on watching as the man, shirtless in the heat, began to squirm and fidget under the car. *Ants,* Baldwin said to himself. *Might as well let him lie there a minute.*

Baldwin then heard the sound he had been waiting for— the low, menacing growl of two Dobermans. The fugitive hadn't noticed—even though he used it for a foothold—the large red sign on the fence: Guard Dogs on Duty.

An Ice Guy

Officer Ernest Burt was executing a search warrant for an armed robber and going through the Birmingham, Alabama, house for the third time when he happened to look up and notice that a square of the false ceiling had been moved. Aha!

Right below the ceiling square was a large chest-style freezer, so Burt stepped up onto it to have a look up past the ceiling. Then he thought, *Wait a minute.* He stepped down off the freezer and opened the lid. Gotcha! The man he was looking for was sitting there with his arms wrapped around his legs, rocking back and forth. His skin had turned ashen, and his lips were blue.

"He'd been in there a good twenty minutes," Burt remembers. "If he'd sat in there for another twenty minutes he might have died. He was really very lucky."

Burt took Mr. Freeze out of the freezer and put him in the cooler.

His skin had turned ashen, and his lips were blue.

62 Safety First

As a police officer in Baltimore, Maryland, during the sixties, Frank Walmer ran into his share of dumb criminals, including one who had a penchant for robbing mom-and-pop grocery stores. His weapon of choice was a sawed-off shotgun.

"It looked like an oversized handgun, but it was an old-fashioned twelve-gauge with a hammer," Walmer remembers. "There was nothing left of the stock except the pistol grip, and the barrel was no more than six inches long. It didn't even have a trigger guard. This guy hadn't shot anyone yet, but he was getting bolder with each robbery. We figured it was just a matter of time before someone got hurt."

It happened at the very next robbery. Picking out a small grocery store on the west side of town, he came charging through the door, like Jesse James, waving his sawed-off shotgun and making everyone lie on the floor. He scooped up the few dollars in the register, then

He came charging through the door, like Jesse James, waving his sawed-off shotgun.

backed out the door, sweeping the shotgun back and forth and glaring menacingly at the terrified elderly owner and his equally frightened wife. Pausing in the door for dramatic effect, he aimed the shotgun at the trembling man and said, "Old man, I'm leaving now. And you better not call the cops for ten minutes, or I'll come back and kill you."

Wide-eyed with terror, the man nodded.

"You understand what I'm talking about?" the robber shouted.

"Yes," the owner managed to croak.

"Yes, what?" the bad guy said, cocking the hammer.

"Yes, sir," the man squeaked.

The robber smiled. "That's better. Now don't move, and no one will get hurt." With that, he jammed the shotgun into his belt, catching the trigger on his pants and causing the weapon to discharge.

"Me and one of the sergeants got there at the same time," Walmer says. "We found the guy lying on the ground, moaning. The sergeant examined the wound, and the guy asked him if he was going to die. The sergeant shook his head and said, 'No, you're not going to die. But when you get out of prison, you might want to try for a job with the Vienna Boys Choir.' "

No Brain, No Gain

63

Police on a stakeout in North Carolina observed a man breaking into a transmission shop by smashing in and climbing through a back window. The police rushed in to arrest him, only to discover that he had broken into a restroom that provided no entry into the building. In a rare instance of the dumb criminal getting a break, the man could not be charged with breaking and entering—because the restroom door hadn't been locked. He was charged with destruction of property.

64 Three Days of the Convict

Officer Kevin Studyvin of the Birmingham (Alabama) Task Force tells of the time he and his partner were working on a Saturday afternoon, wearing plain clothes and operating out of an unmarked car. As they pulled up to a red light, Studyvin noticed a familiar-looking man on the other side of the intersection. The man across the way made eye contact and began to wave as if he wanted them to pull over. So they did.

"I know you guys are cops, and Saturday must be your day off," he said, "so I figure y'all must be over here in the neighborhood wanting to have a little fun. I've got what you need right here. Y'all want somethin'?"

"Let's do it," Studyvin said, glancing at his partner.

So they did a deal right there.

"We handed him the money, he handed us the dope, and we arrested him," Studyvin says. "No wonder he looked so familiar. We had just busted him for selling us cocaine . . . on Wednesday!"

The Jewel Fool 65

It was late in the afternoon when a seventy-five-year-old woman entered the Las Vegas, Nevada, police station accompanied by her thirty-five-year-old boyfriend. She was dressed nicely and spoke in a quiet tone as she spoke to an officer about a robbery that had just occurred. Her diamond jewelry was missing.

"If you'll step over to this counter, I'll be glad to take your report," said Carolyn Green, the clerk at the front desk. "Your friend will have to sit over there, though, because only one person at a time is allowed in this area."

The woman's young male companion complied and took a seat in one of the chairs against the waiting-area wall.

"You were robbed, ma'am?" Green asked.

"Yes, I was," she replied. "At my house . . . about ten thousand dollars' worth of diamonds was taken from my house."

After taking down the rest of the necessary information

to start the paperwork, Green asked the woman, "Do you have any idea who it was that robbed you?"

"Yes, I do," came the response.

"Do you know the person's name?"

"Yes, I know his name."

"Would you know him if you saw him again?"

Again, the answer was in the affirmative.

"Do you know where the person is and where we might be able to find him right now?"

The elderly woman looked over her shoulder. "He's sitting right over there against the wall," she said, pointing to her male companion. Green stood up and looked over at the man who had just brought the woman to the station.

"*He's* the man who robbed you?" Green asked in shocked disbelief.

"Yep. My jewels were missing, and I told him I was going to go down to the police station to report it. I asked him to come along, and he said yes, he'd even give me a ride down here. So he did, and here we are."

Green shook her head and called over to the young man. "Sir, will you step over here, please?" The man stood and walked over to the counter.

"Yes?" he said nonchalantly.

"Did you steal this woman's jewelry?"

"I did," he said.

"One moment please, sir," the clerk said. She turned to summon an officer. "This man just admitted that he robbed this woman of ten thousand dollars' worth of jewelry, and now she's signing a complaint against him."

The summoned officer shook *his* head. "Didn't you just come in here with her?"

"Yes," the young man answered blankly.

"She says you're responsible for her missing jewelry."

"She's right," he admitted. "I did it."

"Well, then, you're under arrest for robbery," the still-stunned officer told him.

"Okay," the man sighed, placing his hands over his head and surrendering without incident. He was later sent to prison.

The police probably could have recovered plenty of rocks had they been able to open the man's head.

Brown-Bagging It

At about noon on a sultry North Carolina summer day, homicide investigator Darryl Price tells us, hundreds of motorists observed a man walking along a busy six-lane highway wearing a brown paper bag over his head, creating a hazard as he stumbled in front of traffic. Motorists used their car phones to alert police.

The man eventually entered a bank and began to shout. Several tense seconds went by. Someone finally asked, "I'm sorry, what did you say?" With no mouthhole, the bag-it bandit could not be understood.

Apparently very nervous, the man constantly turned his head, trying to watch everyone in the room. However, his bag did not turn with his head, so most of his time was spent realigning his eyeholes and, of course, repeating himself.

Money in hand, the robber stumbled blindly into six lanes of lunchtime traffic, narrowly avoiding being run down. He was quickly bagged by police.

He stumbled in front of traffic. Motorists used their car phones to alert police.

161

67 Don't I Know You from Somewhere?

Lt. Kirk Williams of the Randall County Sheriff's Department in Canyon, Texas, ran into a dumb criminal who apparently thought everyone's memory was as bad as his. This fellow walked into a store one morning and paid for his purchase with a check. The clerk took the required information from the man's driver's license, plus his phone number. After completing the transaction, he put the check in the register.

An hour later the check casher was back, this time with a knife. He proceeded to rob the store and make his escape. But he had made no attempt to alter his appearance, and the clerk had no trouble remembering him. When deputies arrived on the scene, not only was the victim able to furnish a good physical description, he also handed over the check with the man's complete identification information.

Needless to say, when the bad guy made it home he was shocked to find the deputies already there waiting for him.

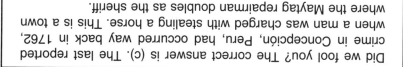

DUMB CRIMINAL QUIZ NO. 602

How well do you know the dumb criminal mind?

In Concepción, Peru, townspeople were recently shocked when a man was accused of stealing two chickens. Was it because:

a) **The same man had been arrested only an hour earlier for the same crime?**
b) **There was only one chicken living in Concepción at the time?**
c) **It was the first reported crime since 1762?**
d) **Stealing a chicken is a capital offense in Peru?**

Did we fool you? The correct answer is (c). The last reported crime in Concepción, Peru, had occurred way back in 1762, when a man was charged with stealing a horse. This is a town where the Maytag repairman doubles as the sheriff.

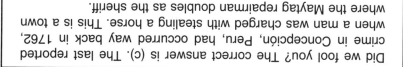

163

68 "Don't Call the Police"

Officer Timothy Walker of the Birmingham (Alabama) Task Force let America's Dumbest Criminals in on one of his personal favorites:

"I was working the eleven-to-seven shift at the time. After running a few errands that morning, I got home around one in the afternoon and went in to get some sleep. I'm lying there on the bed about half-asleep when I hear the sound of glass breaking in the living room.

"I sleep with my gun right next to the bed, so it was already in my hand as I cautiously slipped down the hallway. I heard more glass break as I spun around the corner. I'm just five feet from the window when I see the top of this head and shoulders comin' in. By the time he gets his hands on the floor and looks up, he's staring right down the barrel of my loaded .38.

"He went cross-eyed for a moment. Then I reached out and grabbed him by the shirt with my free hand, and in one swift pull I dragged him into the house."

164

"Don't shoot me! Please don't shoot me!" the burglar cried, perhaps remembering that old adage that says if you shoot somebody on your property, you'd better drag 'em into the house.

"I'm not going to shoot you," Walker told the frightened man, "but you're damned lucky that I didn't!"

"Don't call the police," the man pleaded. "Please don't call the police."

Walker just stared at him. The brilliant break-in artist obviously hadn't noticed the framed photos of Walker in uniform placed on a nearby table . . . or Walker's police cap in a chair . . . or the police badge on his belt . . . or the police-issue firearm nestled in Walker's hand.

"Man, look around," Walker said. "I *am* the police!"

69 "My Life Is Over"

Officer Gordon Martines of the Las Vegas (Nevada) Police Department was running radar one afternoon when he clocked a car at fifty miles per hour in a thirty-five zone. After Martines pulled the car over, the driver got out and walked back to the officer waving his hands in frustration. "My life is over!" the man sighed.

Martines responded, "Well, you were only doing fifteen over the limit. I wouldn't consider that life threatening at this time. May I see your driver's license, please?"

"It's been suspended," the man said.

"Then may I see your vehicle registration?"

"The car is stolen."

"All right, then. Do the license plates belong to the car?"

"The tags are stolen."

"Well, let me see if I've got this straight," Martines said, writing the ticket. "You're speeding on a revoked driver's license, the car is stolen, the tags are stolen, and you have no registration or insurance. I'm going to have to agree with you. Your life *is* over."

Funky Footwork

70

Pensacola, Florida, police officer Marsha Edwards was dispatched along with another marked unit to respond to a disturbance call one afternoon in a usually quiet neighborhood. The officers arrived at the location and were walking up to the door when a man came out brandishing a pistol. The officers scattered across the yard looking for the nearest cover. They drew their weapons and ordered the guy to drop his gun and lie down on the ground—which he did.

"There's three guys still fighting upstairs," he told the officers. So Officer Edwards and two other cops cautiously entered the home while a fourth officer handled the man in the yard.

As soon as they got through the door, they heard scuffling and shouts coming from upstairs. They quickly ran up the steps and found three men punching and kicking each other in a writhing heap on the floor.

Officer Edwards grabbed the first man she could get

her hands on. "I wrestled him to the ground and placed my foot on him between his shoulder and neck and told him to stay put." Meanwhile, the other cops were trying to break up the fight between the other two men.

"Lady, please," the man on the ground pleaded.

"Be quiet and stay still," Edwards told him sternly.

"But lady—"

"Just shut up and lie there," she countered, her foot still pressing down on him.

"Oh, lady, lady, please—"

"What?" she finally shouted at the man. "What do you want?"

"You've got dog poop all over the bottom of your shoe!"

The officer lifted her foot. "Ooooh, you're right. Sorry about that. I must've picked it up out in the front yard. Man, that's nasty."

"That's what I've been trying to tell you," he moaned.

All four men were then arrested for disturbing the peace. For the poor guy on the floor, it turned out to be a pretty crappy day all the way around.

The Couple Who Speeds Together . . .

71

Deputy Sheriff George Korthas of the Oswego County Sheriff's Department in the state of New York knows there are times when honesty is not always the best policy, particularly when it comes to exceeding the speed limit.

Working a radar detail one afternoon, he stopped a woman driver who was doing forty-six in a thirty-mile-per-hour zone. As the woman's car came to a halt, Deputy Korthas noticed another one pull in behind his patrol car. The male driver jumped out and hurried over to Korthas.

"Why are you stopping us?" he asked.

"I'm not stopping *you*," Korthas said. "I'm stopping the woman in this other car."

"I understand that, but we're traveling together, and I'm sure we were going the same speed."

Korthas told the man to stay by his auto while he

talked to the woman. She told him that the man in the second car was her husband and that they were indeed traveling together.

As it turned out, Deputy Korthas had clocked only the first car on radar and didn't have any proof that the second vehicle had been exceeding the speed limit. But always willing to listen to both sides, he walked back to the man standing impatiently beside his car.

Korthas told the guy he had stopped his wife for speeding but had not gotten a radar reading on his car. "Are you *sure* you were traveling the same speed as your wife?"

Clearly irritated, the man said, "Of course, I'm sure. I was right behind her. We were definitely traveling at the exact same speed."

"And what was that speed?" Korthas asked. Becoming more exasperated by the minute, the man threw up his hands and said, "I don't know, probably forty-five, maybe fifty."

Korthas said it took only a few minutes longer to write two tickets instead of one.

Otis Takes a Shortcut

72

Officer Brad Burris of the Pensacola (Florida) Police Department once answered a drunk-driver call at a local go-go club late one night, only to find the driver still in the parking lot—sort of. The way the club parking lot was designed, you could see the interstate below, but you had to drive out of the lot and down to the road to get there. Otherwise, there was an eight- to ten-foot drop-off.

When Burris pulled up in his cruiser, he saw that the two front wheels of the drunk's car were hanging in midair over the edge of the parking lot. He had gotten stuck trying to take a shortcut. The rear end of the car was still on the pavement, the back tires still running at about sixty miles per hour producing clouds of blue smoke.

"I walked up to the driver's-side window, and there behind the wheel was a man who looked just like Otis Campbell from *The Andy Griffith Show*," Burris says. "He was steering with both hands on the wheel and was, for all he knew, driving down the highway. His arms were rockin' a little, and he was staring intensely out the windshield. I mean, this guy was drivin'!"

Burris knocked on the window. The man gave a quick look to his left and went back to his driving, then jerked his head back left and jumped up out of his seat.

"Hey! What the . . . ?" he shouted, wide-eyed and be-wildered, as if he couldn't understand how someone without a car could be running alongside him while he cruised down the highway.

"Pull over," Burris told him. The drunken man blinked widely and complied. He shut off the engine.

"Was I speeding, officer?" the man slobbered.

"Probably. Step out of the car, please."

It was all Burris could do to keep from laughing. "This guy was so drunk that he still didn't get it. As it turned out, he was a really nice guy; he'd just had too much to drink that night. Way too much." He was arrested for D.U.I.

The Draped Crusader

73

This in from Detective B. A. Treadaway of Birmingham, Alabama:

"It was a wild night! We were serving a warrant on a man at this house, and there were several people in the home at the time of the arrest. As soon as we entered, we could smell drugs. They'd been smoking pot and crack and God knows what else. We arrested the man and his friends.

"So we've got this guy handcuffed, and we're reading him his rights when he just takes off running toward the window. Now, this is a big guy, and he's flyin' on something, and he hits that window full force with his hands cuffed behind him. Clears the window out. I mean he shattered the wood, he shattered the glass. He even took the curtain with him—it was flapping in the air."

What our fool had forgotten was that the house was built on a hill, and the particular window he was in the process of jumping out of was two stories off the ground.

Treadaway and crew went running over to the window, sure that the cuffed crusader had just made his final curtain call.

"He's dead," said one of the officers, looking at the ground below.

"I was about to agree with him when this guy gets an adrenaline shot," Treadaway says. "I mean, something must've kicked in, because he jumped straight up and took off running again. Unbelievable. So the chase was on. We all scrambled outside and went running after him. I was thinking to myself, *What if we catch this guy?*"

So Treadaway and his cohorts took off in hot pursuit of the fugitive, who apparently was unaware that he was running straight toward a ten-foot drop-off. This guy didn't slow down a step. Off the ledge he went, with the curtain still flowing like a cape. And as if matters weren't already bad enough, there was a tall tree standing near the edge of the drop-off.

Crash! Our man hit the tree and snapped off a limb. *Thud!* He hit the ground and lay still.

"He's dead now," one of the officers said. But to the officers' amazement, the guy started to get up again as they moved in on him. "I'm not going to run anymore," he said.

"*Well, that's fine with me,* I thought," says Treadaway. "So we walked him back to the house, where a crowd of about ten people had gathered in the front yard, with more in the street. Some were cheering, some were boo-ing. The cheers were for him. His buddies were all talkin' trash and trying to stir something up."

"They pushed him out the window!" one of them yelled, pointing to the vacant frame. "Yeah, I saw it all, the cops threw him out that window up there."

But before the officers could even respond, the caped crusader spoke. "No, they didn't! I jumped out the win-dow myself," he told the mob. "They didn't push me out."

After his head started to clear up, this guy was so thankful to be alive that he even apologized to the offi-cers for running away and causing so much trouble.

Through a Glass Dumbly

The Picture Window Flasher was notorious in Pensacola, Florida. He'd skulk around one of the numerous apartment buildings in town until he found a target he liked, then he'd expose himself through the window. Despite the fact that he left numerous fingerprints (and other smudges) on the windows, he had always managed to elude capture.

Detective Chuck Hughes, then a rookie, spotted Flasher one summer night behind an apartment complex. Hughes called for backup, and Flasher was soon apprehended. He was wearing nothing but a house key on a chain around his neck.

"Please take me by my house first," he begged as they were about to take him downtown. "I don't want to go to jail in the nude!"

The officers were kind enough to oblige him, and he was dumb enough to oblige them with another crime to charge. When they opened the front door to his house, they found a large mirror strewn with razor blades and a big pile of cocaine.

Will the Last Person to Steal the Truck Please Turn off the Lights?

75

It had been snowing in Birmingham, Alabama, for a couple of days—a rare experience for that southern city. Officer Eric Griffin and his partner were patrolling near the railroad tracks by the switching station. It was pretty well deserted except for a couple of railroad workers sitting in a utility truck.

"They must've been doing some kind of maintenance work, because the two yellow bi-lights on the top of the truck were on," Griffin says.

The officers drove past the men and proceeded to the end of the road, where they then turned around. As they were heading back they came upon the two workers, now on foot. But there was no sign of the truck.

"They just stole my truck!" one of the men shouted.

"Who stole your truck?" the officers asked.

"Two men. We were checking for loose rails, and when I looked up there were these two guys gettin' into the truck, and they just took off! It's a blue Chevy pickup with the yellow lights on top. They hit the main road and went east toward town."

The two officers dropped the two men off at the brakeman's shack and rolled. As they got into town, they passed a housing project on their right.

"There they are!" Griffin's partner suddenly yelled. Griffin looked over. Sure enough, there was the truck, with the yellow bi-lights still flashing away. The officers turned into the projects and had to make several twists and turns in order to get over to where they'd seen the lights. When they got there, the truck was gone. But then Griffin's partner spotted it again. "There they go, the next street over!"

As the officers turned at the next street, the truck passed directly in front of them. The bi-lights were still flashing. One of the men was kicking frantically on the dash and holding a fistful of wires. He still hadn't found the off switch. Finally, with the help of another unit, Griffin and company were able to trap the vehicle and make the arrest.

"As we were taking the passenger out of the truck, I couldn't help myself," Griffin recalls. "I reached in and turned off the lights."

178

One of the men was kicking frantically on the dash and holding a fistful of wires.

76

The Car Dealer, the Card Dealer, and Mom

One crazy story told by Officer Bruce Harper and still making the rounds among Las Vegas, Nevada, police officers concerns two brothers and their seventy-year-old mother who stopped by a car dealership in Las Vegas. They asked the salesman if they could test-drive a particular new car. He threw a set of tags on it, climbed in the backseat, and they were off.

After they'd gone a few miles, one of the men asked his brother to pull over so he could drive the car. When they stopped, they ordered the salesman out of the backseat and forced him into the trunk. Then they shut the lid and headed out of town.

Another motorist had witnessed the entire event. He followed them to a casino outside of Vegas and phoned the police. The officers arrived and freed the shaken salesman, who was able to give them a good description of his unlikely kidnappers.

The officers couldn't be sure just how many people might actually be involved, so they acted with caution. A S.W.A.T. team was dispatched to the scene. The team entered the casino and went directly to the security room filled with closed-circuit television monitors. Moments later they spotted one of the brothers seated at a blackjack table.

To apprehend him and the rest of his family, several members of the S.W.A.T. team dressed up like waiters and carried towels and drink trays concealing their weapons. Three of the disguised officers came up behind the brother who had been spotted. Surrounding the guy, they pulled him straight back off his chair and onto the floor. No one else at the table looked up. They were too interested in their card game to care about anything else, but that's Vegas.

Meanwhile, other members of the team had located and arrested the remaining brother. With both brothers now in custody, the focus was on Mom. They'd gotten her name from her sons, so catching her was simply a matter of paging her on the casino intercom system.

The three were charged with grand theft auto and kidnapping. Why an entire family would kidnap a total stranger, put him into the trunk, and then stop to gamble is beyond logic. But then, these weren't exactly the Waltons.

77 Out of the Frying Pan, into the Line of Fire

It was a moonless, balmy Pensacola, Florida, night, and there he was—a criminal fleeing on foot and feeling pretty good about his chances of making the next street and therefore slipping into the anonymous darkness.

Suddenly, behind him, came the screech of tires and the unmistakable flash of a police cruiser's lights. What to do? He knew the neighborhood well, having cased most of the houses during his career.

The next house on the left, he thought. *It's just that little old lady living alone. I'll bust in there. She won't be hard to deal with. After the heat's off, I'll help myself to her jewelry box and get out.*

He ran to the front porch and heaved himself against the front door. No luck. Again he rammed the door with his shoulder. Again it didn't budge. A step back, a swift kick, and the door finally flew open. He slipped inside the door and closed it.

Did they see me? If they did, I'll just take the old bag hostage.

From the darkened hallway came the distinctive sound of a twelve-gauge, pump-action shotgun being readied for use. A southern lady's delicate voice rose quite calmly from the shadows: "You might have better luck with those policemen outside, young man. If you move anywhere but out that door, I'll just have to blow your head off."

The patrolmen who had seen the idiot burglar-to-be enter the house reported that his exit was much faster and that he seemed rather relieved to see three policemen there to save him.

78 Dumb and Semi-Stupid

Veteran female police officer Alson Dula told America's Dumbest Criminals this story about a man who, by any known standard, just has to be one of, well, one of America's dumbest criminals.

Officer Dula was on patrol in the lovely and historic town of Davidson, North Carolina, when she noticed that the man who just passed her had expired plates on his car. She hit the lights and with a quick blip of the siren pulled him over.

Dula ran the tag number. Not only were the tags expired, but they also didn't belong to the car. The man's driver's license had been revoked as well. She arrested him on those charges.

Exactly one month later to the day, the same man drove through town. Same car. Same tags. Same revoked license. Same officer. He was arrested on the same charges. He again went to jail, made bond, and was awaiting trial when one month later he decided to rob a department store.

He held a knife in his right hand and a newspaper in his left as he approached the counter, putting the newspaper in front of his face as he asked the clerk to hand over all the money in her drawer. She couldn't see his face, but then he had no way of noticing that the clerk was writing down the company name stitched on the blue work shirt the man was wearing, along with his name—which happened to be spelled out above his pocket. You know what comes next: He was found guilty of armed robbery and sentenced to prison.

One month later this guy broke out of jail at night and stole a Mack tractor-trailer truck, minus the trailer. Now he was a free man, so where did he go? Back to town, of course. The police spotted him in the stolen truck, and the chase was on. He was running from one county to another in that Mack truck and soon he had ten cop cars lined up behind him.

Eventually, he decided to drive by the trailer park where his mom lived. She was looking out her trailer window when she saw him go by, still honking the air horn with the squad cars in his wake. "Look, Ma, no brains!"

From there he drove over to the next county, where he and his wife lived in another trailer park. Doing about forty miles an hour, he drove the stolen Mack truck across his front yard and slammed the semi into the front door of his trailer. Then he jumped out of the truck and ran inside.

"Honey, I'm home!" She wasn't. His wife had been informed of his escape and had gone to stay in the neighbor's trailer, from where she watched the whole thing in numb horror.

Police were everywhere—local, state, and county. They surrounded the mobile home and cut off the power to his trailer. Approximately forty-five minutes later, our dumbbell cracked. He walked out of what was left of his trailer with his hands up and surrendered to the anxiously awaiting police. He is now serving his old and new sentences in the penitentiary.

Originality Counts

According to Charlotte, North Carolina, patrolman T. C. Owen, a man trying to explain the presence of his fingerprints at several different crime scenes insisted that "someone has been going around town, using my fingerprints."

80 High-Tech Bomb Threat

It's entirely possible for even high-tech bad guys to be dumb criminals—as in the case of the Florida teenager who decided to use a fax machine to make a bomb threat to his high school.

Although it might have been a stupid idea—even *he* knew that the phone number of the originating fax machine is automatically printed on the fax—this young genius wasn't about to use his own machine. His unbeatable idea would be to use another fax machine and a toll-free number that he had been told could not be traced.

He called a large computer company and asked the person answering for technical assistance. One of the services the company provided was a computer faxing service. The customer could type in a fax number, and the information would be automatically transmitted to that number. Of course, the customer was also expected to put his name on the message. But the kid was too smart for that. In the message box intended for the sender's name, he typed a long message about a bomb being in the high school, along with a few other threats. He then typed in the fax number of his high school, transmitted the message, and quickly disconnected. Immensely pleased with himself, he sat back to see what sort of chaos would transpire.

Unbeknownst to the young man, most of his message was lost in transmission. Because the name box accepts a total of only twenty characters (including spaces), all that went through were the words, "There is a bomb in—"

The school authorities called the cops and, when they arrived, turned over the fax. Lo and behold, it contained the toll-free number of the computer company's technical support line. From there, it was a simple matter for the company to check its records and find where the call had originated.

Within a half-hour the young prankster was in custody. In the presence of his parents, he was soon confessing all and was eventually charged with making the bomb threat. Sadder but wiser after being expelled, the young computer whiz learned that a little knowledge can indeed be a dangerous thing.

Buried Treasure

Retired Escambia County (Florida) Sheriff's Department captain Don Parker knows that modern-day pirates still sometimes bury their loot in the sand. He has some firsthand experience in the matter.

It happened on a quiet summer's night on Pensacola Beach, as Parker and reserve deputy David Stanley were patrolling in Parker's unmarked car. Traffic was light, and there were plenty of tourists and locals walking around enjoying the balmy evening breezes.

As they approached a stop sign, Parker noticed a car behind them in the other lane and coming up fast. To his surprise, the vehicle, a rusted and battered four-door sedan, shot through the intersection, ignoring the stop sign. Unfortunately, a Volkswagen bug was in the wrong place at the wrong time, and the larger car broadsided the VW, spinning it around like a top.

"Luckily, there were no injuries," Parker says, "but it all happened so fast we didn't have time to react."

After the sounds of breaking glass and screeching tires subsided, the two officers jumped out to render aid. Then a strange thing happened.

"The guy sitting on the passenger side of the big sedan came out of the car like a jack-in-a-box, ran to the side of the road, and began digging a small hole," Parker recalls. "David and I watched in amazement as he pulled two sandwich bags full of marijuana from his pocket, dropped them in the hole, and quickly covered the dope with sand.

"Now, it's true we were driving a plain car, but both of us were in full uniform and no more than ten feet from where the man was digging in the sand. Apparently, though, he didn't see us."

Satisfied that the damning evidence had been successfully hidden, the guy casually strolled back to the accident scene. Parker told Stanley to go and stand on the spot where the dope had been buried. Then he went to direct traffic until a trooper could arrive to work the wreck.

A highway patrolman was soon on the scene, and the driver of the sedan freely admitted that he had run the stop sign. Both he and his passenger were friendly and cooperative, and the investigation was quickly completed. The trooper wrote a citation to the at-fault driver, then closed his notebook. "Well," he said to Parker, "I guess that does it."

He pulled two sandwich bags full of marijuana from his pocket, dropped them in the hole, and quickly covered the dope with sand.

192

Parker smiled. "Not quite." He nodded at Stanley, who quickly dug up the two little bags and held them up for everyone to see. "We found some buried treasure, and I think we know who buried it."

The two dumb (and dumbfounded) criminals were quickly handcuffed and placed in the back of Parker's car for the short trip to the beach jail.

82 A Self-Inflicted Drive-By

Drive-by shootings are the scourge of lower-income neighborhoods. Gangs use this cowardly and costly practice to retaliate against enemies and rival gangs—with deadly effect on innocent children and adults who just happen to be in the wrong place at the wrong time. Drive-bys also escalate the cycle of violence as one act of revenge replaces another. But we did hear of a drive-by shooting in Oklahoma that ended with some poetic justice for a change.

A carload of gang members had set out to avenge their honor by taking a few potshots at their rivals on a city street. Their car was a "low rider" loaded down with six young gang members. They cruised the dark night streets, patrolling their "turf" and searching for some stragglers from another gang.

Finally, they spotted their prey—three kids walking

and apparently not aware of the car behind them. The setup was perfect. Nobody else was on the street. All was quiet, no stores were open, and no cops were anywhere to be seen. The cruising shooters cut off their headlights, killed the radio, and silently idled up the street, barely moving.

Just as the shooter in the backseat was ready to pull the trigger, the car's front right wheel rolled into a huge pothole. The car bounced, the gun fired, the front left tire blew, and the young men on the sidewalk scattered. The driver gunned the engine and rode the rim for about half a block; then the wheel came off the axle and the car screeched to a grating stop. The gunman inside the car had foolishly shot out his own tire.

When the police arrived to apprehend the gang members, they found them arguing and fighting amongst themselves over the flat tire.

No Fair

Detective John Crain of Birmingham, Alabama, and his partner were working undercover, doing drug buys and arresting prostitutes. One night they happened to be down by the state fairgrounds, when a citizen flagged them down.

"I been seein' y'all out here cruisin' around," the man said. "Guess you must be workin' at the fair. I just wanted to let y'all know that I can get you anything you want. Anything! I can get you drugs, prostitutes, housing—you name it. I'm the man to see."

Not wanting to pass up a good opportunity, Crain asked the man, "Can you get us some crack?"

"No problem, man; just run me down the street here."

So Crain and his partner gave him a lift to a certain house, where he went in to get the drugs. Then he said, "Hey, I've got two women in my motel room. Let's go over there and do some partyin'."

"So we take this guy over to this sleazy motel and go

into the room," Crain says. "But instead of two women waiting there, we met three more men."

This changed everything. Suddenly, the odds were four to two, and the officers had no backup. Crain and his partner didn't know if this was a setup or how many of these guys had weapons or what. So they just continued to play along.

"Hey, let's smoke some of that rock you just got," one of the men finally said to Crain.

"I want to wait for the girls," Crain coolly answered. "We'll smoke it when they get here, and then we'll go get some more."

"We don't have to go get more," one of the others said. "We've got plenty right here."

At that point, everybody started pulling out rocks of cocaine. They were arguing with each other about who had the best stuff. It was definitely time to end the party.

"Police officers!" Crain yelled. "Everybody freeze!"

"This was a tense situation," Crain remembers. "At any moment, one of them could have pulled a gun and started shooting. I'm thinkin', *We need some backup,* but I didn't know how we could call for backup without the means to do so. It was a standoff for a minute. Then I took hold of my collar and began talking into one of the buttons on my lapel."

"Hold your positions; we are in control!" Crain barked

"Hold your positions; we are in control!" Crain barked into his, uh, microphone.

198

into his, uh, microphone. "All units, hold your positions!"

While this charade was going on, Crain's partner managed to slip out of the room and call for real backup. All of the men were arrested.

Says Crain, "The one who thought we worked at the fair asked me later, 'What was that button you were talkin' into? Man, you guys are comin' up with some neat stuff nowadays.'

"*Yeah,* I thought, *we sure are.*"

84 When You're Right, You're Right

Traffic violations tend to stimulate creativity, engendering some of the most original excuses ever thought of, and all cops have their favorites. Former Baltimore, Maryland, police officer Frank Walmer remembers one of the best excuses he ever heard.

"I was dispatched to handle a traffic accident at the corner of Mulberry and Carey," he says. "When I got there I found five bent and battered cars but no serious injuries. Of course, things were pretty confused, with angry drivers milling around, a big crowd of people, and a major traffic snarl."

Walmer set to work trying to untangle the situation, but the job took quite awhile. "After awhile I noticed a man standing off to one side, wearing a tuxedo. As I walked over to talk to him, several of the drivers said that he was the one who had caused the wreck by running a red light."

Ignoring the shouted accusations, the man readily

responded to Walmer's request for a driver's license. He handed it to him with a smile and said, "These people are wrong. I was not at fault."

Walmer told him that at least a half-dozen witnesses had accused him of running the red light.

The man nodded. "Yes, it's true I ran the red light, but I had the right of way."

Officer Walmer asked him how that could be true. He didn't appear to have been driving an emergency vehicle, and that would have been the only way he could claim the right of way in such a situation.

The driver smoothed the lapels of his tuxedo, looked disdainfully at the shouting rabble, then said loftily, "Of course, I had the right of way. I was in a wedding procession."

85 A Bad Hair Day

Officer Bill Cromie of the Oswego County (New York) Sheriff's Department has heard his share of excuses from traffic violators, but one in particular sticks in his mind.

On a warm summer afternoon he was working a traffic detail when he saw a car approaching at a pretty good clip.

"There was a young man driving, and I was struck by the fact that he was driving with his head hanging out the window like a cocker spaniel," Cromie said. "He was also doing sixty-five in a thirty according to my radar, but he stopped right away when I turned on my lights.

"I walked up to the driver's side and noticed that the man's hair was dripping wet. I asked him if there was some kind of medical emergency, but he said there wasn't."

It turned out the young man was on his way to his girlfriend's house and had just washed his hair. Unfortunately, his hair dryer was broken. "I just hate to go over there with wet hair," he said. "So I figured I would just stick my head out the window and let the wind do it for me. I guess I wasn't watching my speed."

Cromie said it was one of the most original excuses he had ever heard, so he let the young man off with a warning. As he was walking back to his patrol car, the now-happy man yelled his thanks, then added, "And I promise I'll get a new hair dryer."

86 O, Please

Las Vegas, Nevada, policeman Sam Hilliard and his partner were on routine red-eye patrol at about three o'clock one morning when they were flagged down by a concerned citizen about a disturbance that was keeping him—and the whole neighborhood—awake. It seems that farther down the street there was a strange man throwing rocks at the neighborhood church and cursing loudly.

After hearing the concerned citizen's story, the officer who was driving stepped on the gas and headed to the church, where he and his partner found a man fitting the citizen's description of the suspect. The officers pulled up alongside the man and asked, "Were you the one throwing rocks at the church?"

"Yes, I was. So what?"

"So why were you doing that?"

"I'm mad at the church!"

"Why are you mad at the church?"

The man launched into a brief explanation having something to do with the church not having a picture of Jesus Christ dying on the cross. And that apparently had made the man angry enough to cast stones.

By this time, the officers had managed to get a good whiff of the rock thrower. It was clear he had been drinking—a lot. The officers weren't about to get into a religious discussion with a drunk, but they felt compelled to exit their cruiser and investigate more closely. After all, this was a public place, and there had been a disturbance.

"We began patting the man down," one of the cops remembers. "Reaching into a large inside jacket pocket, we pulled out this big letter *O*. Of course, we asked him what it was."

"That's my *O*," he replied.

"Your *O*?"

"Yeah, that's my souvenir from the church."

The two officers looked up at the front of the church. Sure enough, the word *Catholic* in the church's main sign was missing its *O*. Told that the *O* rightfully belonged to the church, the man reluctantly consented to giving it back to the officers. They thanked him and told him to be on his way, but not to do any driving.

"After the man left, we returned the big *O* to its place and were in the process of writing the resident priest a note explaining what had happened when this car comes slowly rolling up."

Guess who!

The officers didn't know what to expect. Maybe the guy now had a gun on him. Maybe he had revenge on his mind. No matter. The two officers quickly drew their weapons and ordered the man to stop the car and get out.

"I want my *O*!" the man ranted and raved. "Give me my *O*! It's my *O*!"

It eventually dawned on the officers that the man wasn't armed. But he was still drunk. So they had little resistance when it came to making the arrest.

"Enough was enough," our Vegas friends told America's Dumbest Criminals. "We tried to give him a break the first time, figuring that his anger was between him and God. But when he became a drunk driver, that was between him and us.

"And, *'O'* yeah, we arrested him for D.U.I."

Sprechen Sie Deutsch?

Officer Arnold Hagman of the Boise (Idaho) Police Department was born in Germany and speaks fluent German. Working a traffic detail one day, he stopped a woman for speeding. When he walked up to the car to obtain her driver's license, she gave him a helpless, melting smile and said, in German, that she didn't speak any English.

Officer Hagman was more than just sympathetic. Nodding politely, he said, *"Heute ist ein glücklicher Tag für Sie,"* which means, of course, This is your lucky day.

Evidently, she disagreed, because the smile disappeared much faster than it had appeared.

# **88 Going Down**

Sgt. Ernest Burt of the Birmingham (Alabama) Police Department has served hundreds of arrest warrants in his time. But few have involved cases as bizarre as this one, the moral of which suggests that a criminal's guilt can bear a heavy burden.

One morning, officers approached the door to one of the units in one of Birmingham's oldest apartment buildings and began knocking. They stood there for several minutes patiently rapping away, waiting for a response. Finally, an elderly woman opened the door a crack, revealing a dour expression and saying nothing.

"We have an arrest warrant for a Mrs. Sheryl Tary," Burt said. "Is she at home?"

"No, she's not here," the woman curtly answered.

Burt pressed on, politely telling the woman at the door that he and his partner would like to come in and look around. He was in the process of explaining himself to the uncooperative greeter when, suddenly, they heard a tremendous crashing sound from a room inside.

"I mean it was *loud*," Burt said. "My partner and I quickly looked at each other, pushed open the front door, and rushed inside to see what had happened. When we got to the living room, we couldn't believe our eyes."

There, lying on the ground groaning, was a woman weighing about three hundred pounds, surrounded by and covered with pieces of plaster, some of which were still fluttering to the floor. She had fallen through the ceiling from the attic, where she had been hiding out.

Sheryl Tary, we presume.

"We told her to just lie still," said Burt, who by this time was biting his lip. "We dispatched an ambulance to the scene. Three paramedics carried her off on a gurney. At the time, her condition was quite serious, but after they told us she would be all right, we just had to laugh. I'll bet even *she* laughed about it later."

How well do you know the dumb criminal mind?

What was the greatest number of people ever arrested at one time in a democratic nation? Was it:

a) 806?
b) 421?
c) 1,201?
d) 308?
e) 15,617?

The answer is (e). On July 11, 1988, police in South Korea rounded up and arrested 15,617 demonstrators in one form or fashion protesting that summer's Olympic games in Seoul—before the games had even begun!

A Real Drunk Driver

89

A California police officer told us about the time he was especially worried about the car weaving in front of him. It was nighttime, and the road was not well lit. The driver obviously was having a difficult time staying in his lane. He would drift over the double yellow line to his left, then edge over almost to the ditch on his right. The officer had been behind him for nearly a mile with lights flashing and siren wailing when the man finally made a crude stop on the side of the road. He slumped forward onto the steering wheel as the officer approached his car.

"Sir," the officer said, tapping on the driver's window with his flashlight, "turn the car off for me, and step out of the vehicle, please."

The man was dangerously drunk. As he got out of the car, he staggered back against the fender and slid nearly to the ground. The officer kept him from falling.

"I haven't dren binking, occifer," the man slurred.

"How much have you had to drink tonight, sir?" the officer asked.

"I haven't dren binking, occifer," the man slurred.

"Lying to me isn't going to help you, sir. Now, how much have you had to drink?"

"A couple uh beers," he muttered. "Zat's all."

"A couple of beers? Do you take any medication, sir?"

"No. Not that I know of."

"Not that you know of? I need to see your driver's license, sir."

The man fumbled through his wallet and produced a license. As he handed it to the officer, there suddenly was a terrible crash nearby. Two cars had crashed into one another and been knocked to the side of the road.

"Wait right here!" the officer ordered the drunken man. "Don't you move!"

With that the policeman ran forward to the crash site. He was talking with the people involved in the accident when he suddenly saw the drunk man driving past him at a high rate of speed. "Hey!" the officer yelled at him as the man sped by.

Thirty minutes later the police were at the man's house and had it surrounded. Six or seven squad cars sat out in front, and several officers with guns drawn were positioning themselves around the front yard. They were pounding on the door and shouting, "Police! Open up!"

A still-drunk and very groggy man finally answered the door and was immediately seized by the officers, handcuffed, and arrested.

"Hey, what the hell is goin' on here?" he asked belligerently.

"Where's the car?" the officers demanded to know.

"The what?" he asked. "I've been home all night sleeping."

"Where is the car?"

"It's in the garage, I guess. That's where I usually park it." The man seemed totally befuddled.

"Here it is!" an officer shouted from the now-opened garage.

Sure enough, there it sat. The garage was filled with exhaust fumes. The engine was still running. So were the blue lights on the top of the squad car. The guy was so drunk he hadn't even realized that he'd driven off in the police cruiser instead of his own car.

Never Talk to Strangers

90

Retired police captain Don Parker told America's Dumbest Criminals about a man named Simon Bolivar McElroy. He was having a bad day. After being freed from a Florida jail, where he had served time for a drug conviction, McElroy was on his way to catch a little sun at the beach. More to the point, he was going there to sell four plastic sandwich bags of marijuana. But en route to the beach, McElroy heard a metallic *clunk* when he hit the gas after stopping for a traffic light. The engine in his rusty old van had died.

McElroy grabbed his cigarettes and his lighter, shoved the bags of marijuana down inside his underwear, and walked away from the van, leaving the keys dangling from the ignition. McElroy stuck out his thumb and quickly caught a ride. Although he would miss the van, he didn't want to be anywhere near it when the cops showed up.

His ride took him all the way to the beach. He was

beginning to feel better as he sat on the sand enjoying the warm breezes and the passing bikinis. The bags were making him itch, though, so he transferred them to his front pockets and started walking down the beach, looking for potential customers.

McElroy had just topped a sand dune next to a big hotel when he stopped dead in his tracks. Spread out in front of him were at least a hundred guys who looked just like him, with scraggly beards, long, stringy hair, and pasty-white bodies. They were lying on blankets, throwing Frisbees, or splashing in the surf. It looked like a druggie's family reunion.

He walked over to a couple of likely prospects and casually asked if they'd be interested in purchasing some weed. They not only were interested, but they also wanted to buy his entire supply! They dickered over the price and finally settled on an amount at least three times the going street price.

The guy he had been talking to called several others over, and in no time there was quite a little pile of greenbacks on the blanket beside the marijuana. McElroy started to reach for the money, but the guy stopped him. He told McElroy that they were now permanent friends and that he was going to sign his initials on every single bill as a token of his admiration for McElroy's kindness. Someone produced a pen, and the guy did exactly that.

216

Although McElroy thought this behavior bizarre, he wouldn't have cared if the idiot had danced an Irish jig.

When the last bill had been signed, McElroy was given the money. He was about to take his leave when the guy told him he had some bad news. Before McElroy could react, each of the long-haired spectators suddenly produced a badge. They were of all shapes and colors and represented a variety of local, state, and federal law enforcement agencies.

As he was being escorted to the hotel to await the arrival of a uniformed patrol officer, McElroy was told he had managed to find an entire convention of narcotics investigators, in town to attend a training seminar.

The guy who had marked the bills was one of the instructors. He slapped McElroy on the back and told him to cheer up. "Look on the bright side," he said. "At least we'll have a really great story to start off tomorrow's session."

That Volunteer Spirit

Officer Paul Hickman and two other narcotics officers were searching a pair of crack dealers on a street corner in Charlotte, North Carolina. It was a bright, beautiful day. People were walking the sidewalks, taking in the air. It was the kind of afternoon when anything seemed possible.

As the officers were cuffing the crack dealers, a young man approached them and said, "Hey, do you want to search me?"

It seemed like a setup. No one would just come up out of the blue and offer to be searched if he had anything to hide. But one officer, perhaps enjoying the humor of the gesture, said, "All right" and proceeded to pat him down.

The officer found a bag of crack cocaine in the man's pocket.

"Oh, man," complained the volunteer, "I was just being polite! You weren't supposed to say yes!"

Nothing to Fear but Fear Itself

92

It was about ten at night when Deputy Sheriff Bill Cromie of Oswego County, New York, was dispatched to a traffic accident in the small town of Constantia, New York. Arriving on the scene, he found that a car had crashed into some gasoline pumps and that the intoxicated driver had fled the scene on foot. The rescue squad had foamed the whole area down to prevent a fire, and things seemed to be under control.

Cromie asked if anyone had any idea which direction the missing driver had run. One of the firefighters pointed toward a ravine next to the road. "He ran down there," he said. "He's been crashing around in the woods for the last hour. You can still hear him."

Sure enough, the sounds of something large and clumsy barreling through the foliage, could be plainly heard. The ravine was pitch dark, and Cromie proceeded

219

cautiously down the steep slope, heading toward the sound of snapping branches. As he got closer he could also hear heavy breathing.

He turned on his flashlight. There, illuminated by the beam, was one pitiful human being. Filthy, scraped and scratched, his clothing in tatters and utterly exhausted, the still-drunk driver blinked in the glare.

"Sheriff's Department," Cromie announced. "Are you the driver of that car back there?"

The man slid to the ground, panting heavily, and raised his trembling hands. "I give up," he said. "I was driving, and I thought I could get away through the woods." He shook his head wearily. "You must be Superman."

Cromie asked him what he meant. "Man, you been chasing me for forty-five minutes, and you aren't even winded. Hell, you ain't even messed up the crease in your pants. How did you do it?"

Cromie laughed and told the man that he had only just arrived on the scene and that no one had been chasing him. The drunk let this information sink in for a few minutes, then looked up. "You mean I been chasing myself?"

"I'm afraid so."

The guy struggled to his feet. "Well, if I'm that damn stupid, you might as well put me in jail." Cromie was happy to oblige.

A Doubleheader

93

While on patrol during a midnight shift in Baltimore, Maryland, Officer Frank Walmer spotted a guy walking down the street carrying a television. The man made no attempt to escape as Walmer approached, and he readily furnished identification. He said the television belonged to him. He had recently lent it to a friend and now was taking it home.

"I ran the serial number and had communications check for any recent burglaries involving that brand of TV," Walmer says. "But they found nothing, so I had to let the guy go."

But just before he got off duty, Walmer was dispatched to the scene of a residential burglary and, sure enough, one of the items stolen was a television of the make and model that he had just seen on the street.

"The homeowner was really upset and was running around the living room showing me where all the missing items had been, the broken window where the burglars had gained entry, and the items that might have fingerprints. But the really interesting thing was that on the coffee table, in plain view, were at least three ounces of marijuana, a stack of rolling papers, scales, and several roach clips."

Walmer took all the information furnished by the irate homeowner and then pointed at the dope. "You say they got your television but not your marijuana, is that right?"

The guy nodded. "That's right. They came through the window, got my TV, but left the—" His voice died as he realized what he was about to say. He looked at the dope, looked at Walmer, and then swallowed hard. "I can't believe I left that stuff there," he whispered.

"As I was handcuffing him, I told him the situation wasn't all bleak, because I was pretty sure I would be able to recover his television." And Walmer did just that. Because he had the previous suspect's complete address, Walmer drove to his house and found him sitting in his living room watching the stolen TV.

"All in all," Walmer remembers, "it was a pretty good night."

One for the Road

94

Tampa, Florida, police officer David Shepler has won an award for arresting more drunk drivers in one year than anyone else in his department. His experience and skill stand him in good stead even when responding to routine traffic calls—like the one that took him to the scene of a traffic accident on Interstate 275 near the Tampa airport.

Arriving on the scene, Officer Shepler found a nearly demolished car up against the guardrail of the busy interstate. "The first thing I saw was about three hundred feet of red paint where the car had scraped and skidded all along the guardrail. The next thing I noticed was that the car was still moving—but barely."

Shepler ran to the car and found the driver still behind the wheel, doing his best to drive his wrecked vehicle away. "I told him to turn off the engine, but he said he was in a hurry and had to be someplace. It was then I realized he was heavily intoxicated, so I reached through the window and took the keys."

The driver staggered out of the car and stood by the door, swaying like a sapling in a strong wind. Shepler told him he suspected him of being drunk and was going to give him some roadside sobriety tests. "As soon as I told him this, the guy reached inside the car and hauled out a six-pack of beer. He pulled off two cans and offered me one. I refused it and told him again I was about to administer a roadside sobriety test."

The inebriated driver nodded and said, "Yeah, I heard all that. But I do much better on tests when I've had something to drink."

Needless to say, Officer Shepler had to inform the man that he had had quite enough to drink. The Breathalyzer reading confirmed this, reading his blood alcohol level at .31—which is more than three times the legal limit in Florida.

Watch That First Step

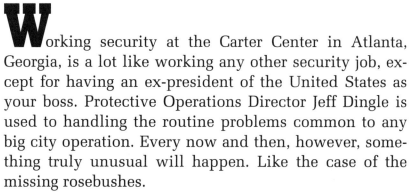

Working security at the Carter Center in Atlanta, Georgia, is a lot like working any other security job, except for having an ex-president of the United States as your boss. Protective Operations Director Jeff Dingle is used to handling the routine problems common to any big city operation. Every now and then, however, something truly unusual will happen. Like the case of the missing rosebushes.

The rose garden at the Carter Center is pleasing to the eye, but the plants are not inexpensive. So Jeff was understandably concerned when a groundskeeper told him that five of the plants had been stolen the previous night. The next day, five more disappeared, and five more the day after that. Because the thefts were obviously occurring after normal business hours, Dingle decided to set up surveillance on the rose garden in hopes of catching the thief.

Well aware that stakeouts can be mind numbingly

Within a few minutes he had dug up three plants while the protective operations director watched.

boring, Jeff was mentally prepared for hours of tedious monotony. For the early hours he decided he could get a good view of the garden by simply sitting on a nearby bench like any other tourist. The center closes at five o'clock in the afternoon, and by that time Dingle was on his bench hoping against hope that the rosebush thief might put in an early appearance.

He didn't have to wait long. At two minutes after five, one of the local crackheads, carrying a small shovel, came around the corner and headed straight for the roses. Within a few minutes he had dug up three plants while the protective operations director watched in amazement.

Realizing he needed to take action, Dingle walked over to the man, identified himself, and asked him what he was doing. The guy threw down the shovel, assured Dingle he wasn't doing a thing, and then turned and ran. Dingle pursued him while calling for assistance on his radio.

Now picture a building built into the side of a hill, with a back roofline only two feet off the ground. The suspect jumped up onto this low-slung roof and headed for the other side with Dingle still in pursuit. Unfortunately for this dumb rose thief, the other end of the roof is twenty-eight feet off the ground, a fact he discovered only when he reached it. He skidded to a stop and looked back to see several security people closing in.

Frantically looking around for an escape route, the thief looked to one side and saw a grassy area leading down to a small lake. Convinced that freedom lay in that direction, he did the dumbest possible thing. He jumped.

Big mistake. The grassy area and lake were some distance away. And directly below the point where he jumped was a concrete sidewalk, which is what the rose thief hit, breaking both legs.

The ensuing excitement, with police cars and an ambulance and lots of uniforms, attracted quite a crowd. As the unfortunate suspect was being loaded into the ambulance, one of the late arrivals asked what the guy had done. Told that the man had stolen a rosebush, he shook his head in amazement.

"I always heard they was tough in Atlanta," he said. "But I didn't know they was that tough!"

Those Small-Town Blues

96

High school graduation night is a time of celebration as one era ends and another begins. Of course, there are always those who have a tendency to overindulge. It was well past midnight when Deputy Bill Cromie of Phoenix, New York, spotted such a future leader of tomorrow driving along the shoulder of the road at fifteen miles an hour.

Cromie loaded up the intoxicated young driver and took him to jail. En route, the kid complained bitterly that Cromie had no right to arrest him because he was a Vietnam veteran who had honorably served his country. Deputy Cromie would have been impressed, except the kid's driver's license indicated he had been born two years after the Vietnam War ended!

Cromie brought the kid inside and sat him down in a chair. The lad sat quietly for a few moments as Cromie worked on his report, but then suddenly shouted, "Don't do that! Stop it! Stop hitting me!" Amused, Cromie ignored him, but the kid kept yelling and then he suddenly kicked backward, tipping over the chair and crashing to the floor. Cromie's sergeant came running and found the still-intoxicated driver lying on the floor.

"Call me an ambulance," the kid wailed pitifully.

Cromie looked up from his report and said, "All right, you're an ambulance."

Cromie then turned to the sergeant and explained what had happened, assuring him there was nothing wrong. The kid, realizing his plan wasn't working, righted the chair and sat in silence while Cromie finished the paperwork.

An hour later Cromie and his prisoner stood in front of the judge. Cromie explained the facts in the case, including the boy's attempt to fake a charge of police brutality. As Cromie finished his narrative the boy turned and snarled, "You're nothing but a small-town cop." The judge cautioned him to refrain from gratuitous insults and was promptly told that he was "nothing but a small-town judge."

The judge smiled. "You may be right, son, but I've got some good news for you. We do have a big-city jail, and you're going to get to spend some time in it."

It Seemed Like a Good Idea at the Time

97

When William S. Meyers was with the Anne Arundel County Police Department in Maryland, he heard about a couple of less-than-intellectual giants who decided they would rob an automatic teller machine.

Of course, our crooks knew they couldn't just walk up to a machine, point a gun at it, and demand money. They knew ATMs are protected by alarms and surveillance cameras: any attempt to break into the machine would likely result in a whole bunch of cops showing up. But they were going to avoid all that because they had a fool-proof plan. They would steal the entire machine.

The scheme was simplicity itself. Late at night they would attach a chain to the ATM, then fasten the chain to the back bumper of their pickup. When everything was secure, they would hit the gas, jerk the machine right out of the wall, and be gone long before the cops arrived on the scene.

They picked a dark and rainy Friday night when the streets were deserted and the ATM was likely to have a fresh supply of money for the weekend. They quietly wrapped the chain around the machine, then tied it securely to the back bumper of their truck. The driver pushed the pedal to the floor, and the pickup shot forward.

Because the ATM appeared to be mounted securely, the would-be thieves had used a heavy chain to make sure it would stand the strain. Unfortunately for them, they had not used a heavy-duty pickup. When the chain snapped taut, it ripped the back bumper right off.

With alarm bells ringing, sirens yelping, and strobe lights flashing, the panic-stricken crooks didn't even slow down, and soon they were far away. Although shaken by the experience, they were happy to escape and even laughed at the thought of the cops arriving to find them long gone.

What they didn't realize was that when the rear bumper was torn off the license plate went with it. It didn't take long for the responding officers to obtain a registration, along with names and addresses. Within the hour, they were adding two more dumb criminals to the large selection already housed in the county jail.

You Snooze, You Lose

98

Detective Dennis Larsen tells us about a pair of high achievers who were fired from their jobs at a Las Vegas, Nevada, car rental agency. Disgruntled, they plotted to rob the manager. They knew the exact time and bank at which the manager made a nightly deposit. So they hatched a plan whereby one of them would lie in wait with a gun and the other would cruise the area on getaway standby.

The first conspirator (we'll call him Heckle) dropped his partner (Jeckle) at the bank about thirty minutes before the manager was due. Jeckle donned a ski mask and took his place behind a Dumpster with a commanding view of the night depository. Heckle set about inconspicuously driving around the block at three miles an hour.

Jeckle waited. Heckle drove. Jeckle got drowsy. Heckle drove. Jeckle fell asleep. The manager made his deposit. Heckle drove. Jeckle slept. Heckle drove.

Police responded to a report of a man sleeping in a ski mask behind a Dumpster and a car out of gas nearby.

K-911

After filling his tank at a Denver, Colorado, gas station, Jeff King decided to rob the station attendant. As King jumped into his car to make his getaway, his one-year-old puppy jumped out to relieve himself. King made several unsuccessful attempts to coax the animal back into the car but eventually was forced to abandon his beloved pet. He knew that, by now, the police were surely on their way.

Within moments of the cops' arrival, the playful pup had become perfectly content to stand still while the officers scratched his ears and read his dogtag, complete with the owner's name and address.

Let's see, if seven years of a dog life equals one human year, the dog should be about fifty when his master gets out of prison.

Only a Phone Call Away

100

As a school resource officer in Tampa, Florida, David Shepler one day was called in to handle a locker theft. A teenage girl reported that twenty dollars and a pager had been stolen from her locker.

School authorities had a suspect, another teenage girl. Officer Shepler questioned her about the theft. She eventually admitted that she had taken the twenty dollars (which she returned) but stoutly denied taking the pager.

After several minutes of fruitless questioning, Shepler told the victim to go to a nearby phone and dial the pager's number. She did as requested. A moment later a strange beeping and clattering sound came from where the suspect was sitting. Concealed in the suspect's underwear, the missing beeper was rattling and vibrating against the metal chair.

"Once that pager went off, it was a little hard for the girl to keep denying she had it," Shepler says, "so that case was soon cleared."

Daniel Butler is a writer, producer, director, and actor who has written and acted in Ernest P. Worrell commercials and movies, children's television, and interactive projects for the National Science Foundation.

Alan Ray is an award-winning songwriter and has written several specials for National Public Radio and American Public Broadcasting.